LEARN ITALIAN FOR BEGINNERS Conversational Italian Dialogues Quick and Easy.Includes Italian Grammar, Italian Short Stories and basic vocabulary for travellers.

Table of Contents

Section (A): Basic Grammar
    INTRODUCTION
    Present Perfect Tense
    Italian Past Perfect Tense
    Remote Past Tense
    Italian Preterite Perfect Tense
    Italian Future Indicative Tense
    Italian Future Perfect Tense
Section (B): Basic Vocabulary for Travelers
Section (C): Italian Dialogues and Sentences
Section (D): Italian Short Story

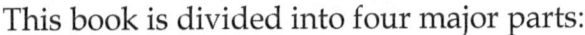

This book is divided into four major parts:
- basic grammar
- basic vocabulary for travellers
- basic conversational Italian Dialogues with particular attention to the pronunciation
- Italian Short and easy Stories

First part contains a concise grammar of Italian organized in the familiar traditional way, describing the forms of Italian in turn. This section should be used for quick reference when you want to know something about a form or structure you can identify

Second part contains the vocabulary terms for travelers or tourists. The vocabulary terms are written taking in consideration, the needs of people whose first language is not Italian . It is organized according to the kinds of words you might want to say in particular situations in Italian, and here you can look up such things as how to apologize, how to ask the time, how to describe a person, etc.

Third part is based upon basic Italian dialogues and sentences which are used in daily routine. It also helps to learn how to pronounce specific terms and words of Italian language.

Fourth part consists of short stories. This part is useful when a person is at least good in Italian grammar and able to understand the combination of words. These short stories are really helpful to give speed flow in Italian Language.

We have not hesitated to use traditional grammatical terms, especially in the first part. It is worth spending a little time getting to grips with these: understanding the terms will help you understand the structures better, even if they may appear a bit daunting at first. We hope that readers will find our approach interesting and useful: we will be delighted to receive opinions on the book and details about the ways in which it has been used in teaching and learning Italian.

Section (A): Basic Grammar

INTRODUCTION

I. Articles.

In English, the definite article (l'articolo determinativo) has only one form: the. In Italian, on the other hand, l'articolo determinativo has different forms according to the gender, number, and even the first letter of the noun or adjective it precedes. It's meant to indicate a precise, quantifiable object or person.

This makes learning definite articles a bit more complicated, but once you know the structure, it's relatively simple to get used to.

il quaderno e la penna - the notebook and pen: In this example, the definite articles are "il" and "la."

i ragazzi e le ragazze - the boys and girls: In this example, the definite articles are "i" and "le."

Here's a table with the definite articles.

	Singular	Plural
Masculine	il, lo, l'	i, gli
Feminine	la, l'	le

Sometimes the articles can be tricky to pronounce (especially "gli").

When to Use Definite Articles

Here is a list of general rules for when to use definite articles.

1. Lo (pl. gli) is used before masculine nouns beginning with s + consonant or z, like "lo zaino - the backpack" or "gli scoiattoli - the squirrels".

You will also see "lo" being used with masculine nouns that begin with "gn," like "lo gnomo."

Here are some examples.

l'orologio—gli orologi >> watch—watches

l'amico – gli amici >> friend—friends

lo yoga >> yoga
lo yogurt >> yogurt

lo specchio—gli specchi >> mirror—mirrors

lo stadio – gli stadi >> stadium—stadiums
lo psicologo – gli psicologi >> psychologist—psychologists

lo zero—gli zeri >> zero—zeros

NOTE: there are a few exceptions:

il dio—gli dèi >> god—gods

per lo meno >> at least
per lo più >> mostly

2. **Il** (pl. i) is used before masculine nouns beginning with all other consonants, like "il cibo - the food" or "i vestiti - the clothes."
3. **L'** (pl. gli) is used before masculine nouns beginning with a vowel, like "l'aeroporto - the airport,"
4. **La** (pl. le) is used before feminine nouns beginning with any consonant, like "la borsa - the purse" or "le scarpe - the shoes."

Here are some examples:

la stazione – le stazioni >> train station—train stations
la zia – le zie >> aunt—aunts
l'amica >> her friend
l'automobile >> the car

5. **L'** (pl. le) is used before feminine nouns beginning with a vowel, like "l'amica - the friend" or "le donne - the women."

The article agrees in gender and number with the noun it modifies and is repeated before each noun.

la Coca-Cola e l'aranciata - the Coke and orangeade
gli italiani e i giapponesi - the Italians and the Japanese
le zie e gli zii - the aunts and uncles
le zie e il nonno - the aunts and the grandfather

The first letter of the word immediately following the article determines the article's form.

Compare the following:

il giorno (the day) → l'altro giorno (the other day)
lo zio (the uncle) → il vecchio zio (the old uncle)
i ragazzi (the boys) → gli stessi ragazzi (the same boys)
l'amica (the girl friend) → la nuova amica (the new girl friend)

Tips When Using Definite Articles

In Italian, the definite article must always be used before the name of a language, except when the verbs parlare (to speak) or studiare (to study) come before the name of the language; in those cases, it's up to you whether you want to use it or not.

Studio l'italiano. - I study Italian.
Studio italiano e arabo. - I study Italian and Arabic.
Parlo italiano. - I speak Italian.
Parlo l'italiano e il russo. - I speak Italian and Russian.
Parlo bene l'italiano. - I speak Italian well.

The definite article is also used before the days of the week to indicate a repeated, habitual activity.

Domenica studio. - I'm studying on Sunday. → Marco non studia mai la domenica. - Marco never studies on Sundays.
Il lunedì vado al cinema (ogni lunedì). - On Mondays, I go to the movies.
On Monday I go to the movies. (Every Monday)
Cosa fai di solito il giovedì? - What do you usually do on thursday evenings?
Di solito vado a giocare a carte con i miei nonni - On thursday, usually I go and play cards with my grandparents.

Finally, another common situation where the definite article is used is with telling the time. Notice here though that the article is combined with a preposition making something called an articulated preposition.

Mi sono svegliato all'una. - I woke up at one.

Vado a scuola alle dieci. - I'm going to school at ten.

You can use it to indicate a category or a species in a generic sense:

Il cane è il miglior amico dell'uomo (tutti i cani). - Dog is man's best friend (all dogs).

L'uomo è dotato di ragione. - Man is endowed with reason. (To talk about "every man")

Or to indicate a particular thing or an object:

Hai visto il film? (quel film) - Have you seen the movie? (that movie)
Hai visto il professore? - Have you seen the professor?

Mi hanno rubato il portafogli. - They stole my wallet.

Non trovo più le scarpe. - I can't find my shoes.

You'll also want to use it when preceding possessive pronouns:

L'auto di Carlo è nuova, la mia no. - Charles's car is new, but mine isn't.

Or with geographical destinations, like:

continents: *l'Europa*
countries: *l'Italia*
regions: *la Toscana*
large islands: *la Sicilia*

oceans: *il Mediterraneo*

lakes: *il Garda*

rivers: *il Po*

mountains: *il Cervino (the Matterhorn)*

And finally, with parts of the body:

Mi fa male la testa.—My head hurts.

Definite Articles with Names

Use definite articles with the last names of famous female celebrities:
la Garbo
la Loren
With all surnames in the plural:
i Verri
gli Strozzi
With nicknames and pseudonyms:
il Barbarossa
il Griso
il Canaletto
il Caravaggio
With proper names used without any specification:
Mario but: il signor Mario
With the last names of famous or well-known male characters, if not preceded by an adjective or title:
Mozart but: il grande Mozart
NOTE: There are instances in which the definite article is used, especially when referring to Italian writers:
il Petrarca
il Manzoni

II. Alphabets

Italian uses the Latin alphabet. In the native words are used only 21 letters and they are considered to form the Italian alphabet properly. There are five vowels, none of which is mute: **a, e, i, o, u**; fifteen consonants: **b, c, d, f, g, l, m, n, p, q, r, s, t, v, z**; and one diacritical letter: h. The latter does not correspond to any sound and is used only to mark half a dozen words in order to distinguish them from similar ones that sound the same but have a different meaning, to mark some interjections, and to mark the velar pronunciation of 'c' and 'g' when otherwise they would be palatalized.

Except for a dozen articles, prepositions and adverbs (that nevertheless are used quite often), all common words in italian end with a vowel; of course this statement does not apply to trade marks, unassimilated foreign words, technical terms, and the like.

Letter	Aa	Bb	Cc	Dd	Ee	Ff	Gg
Letter Name	*a*	*bi*	*ci*	*di*	*e*	*effe*	*gi*

Letter	Hh	Ii	Ll	Mm	Nn	Oo	Pp
Letter Name	*acca*	*i*	*elle*	*emme*	*enne*	*o*	*pi*

Letter	Qq	Rr	Ss	Tt	Uu	Vv	Zz
Letter Name	*cu*	*erre*	*esse*	*ti*	*u*	*vu*	*zeta*

Besides the above mentioned letters; the letters **J, K, X, Y,** and **W** are used only in technical terms and symbols, foreign names, and some very specialized words, such as the international word taxi. J, K and Y survive in toponyms, family names, and english style nicknames, such as Stefy for Stefania (Stephanie). The letter J used to be employed in the past as a graphic device to distinguish the semivowel role of the letter I, so that you have Ajmone (family name) and you may write Iugoslavia (modern spelling), Jugoslavia (old fashioned spelling), or Yugoslavia (international spelling) according to your preference; in italian all three are correct and are pronounced exactly the same way.

Letter	Letter Name	Occurrence

Jj	*i lungo*	Foreign words and names
Kk	*cappa*	Greek words, English and German names
Ww	*doppia vu*	German and English names and words
Xx	*ics*	Greek and Latin words
Yy	*ipsilon*	Greek words, foreign names

PRONOUNCING ITALIAN VOWELS

Italian vowels *(i vocali)* are short, always pronounced very clearly, and are never drawn out. The "glide" with which English vowels frequently end should be avoided. It should be noted that a, i, u, are always pronounced the same way; e and o, on the other hand, have an open and a closed sound that may vary from one part of Italy to the other.

Also, when vowels are grouped together in a word, they are always pronounced separately.

The approximate English equivalents are as follows:
a-A: This letter denotes a single sound, whose pronunciation is always similar to an English a in cat, fact, black; an "o" in how, cloud, house, mouse. Also, It sounds like the word "a" in the English word ah! Examples:
Casa » house.
Amore » love.
Fama » fame.
Pasta » pasta, dough, pastry.
e-E: This vowel has two pronunciations:
As an English "a" in hay, layer, may (this is popularly called a narrow "e" or closed "e")
Bere » to drink.
e » and.
Fede » faith.
Me » me.
As an English "e" in send, met, tent, hen (this one is popularly called a wide "e" or open "e").
Bene » well.
Vento » wind.
è » is.
Festa » party; holiday.

i-I: This vowel always sounds as an English y in yellow, troyan. A similar sound is that of English ee in fleet, seem, but the length of the Italian sound is shorter. Examples:
Invidiare » to envy.
Bimbo » child.
Libro » book.
Vino » wine.
o-O: This vowel has two pronunciations:
Always as an English "o", in some cases with a "narrow" or "closed" sound as in blow, soul, row. Examples:
Dono » gift.
Mondo » world.
Nome » name.
o » or.
Sometimes with a "wide" or "open" sound as in cloth, spot, dog. Examples:
Moda » fashion.
No » no.
Brodo » broth.
Olio » oil.
u-U: This vowel's sound is similar to an English "u" in rule or "w" in win, rowing. But u is a vowel, while w is a consonant. Examples:
Fungo » mushroom.
Luna » moon.
Lungo » long.
Uno » one.

Diphthongs Triphthongs & Word Elision:

In italian a diphthong is formed by any vowel preceded or followed by an unstressed closed vowel ('i' or 'u'):*ia, ie, io, ai, ei, oi, ua, ue, uo, au, eu, ou, iu, ui*. They are always pronounced maintaining the sounds of the individual vowels, and the closed vowel plays the role of a semivowel or a glide.

PRONOUNCING EASY CONSONANTS

Italian has the same consonants that English does. You pronounce some of them the same way, but the rest have noteworthy differences.

Additionally, the modern Italian alphabet has less letters than the English one: J, K, W, X and Y do not occur in native terms. Nevertheless, these letters do appear in dictionaries, for archaic spellings, and for a few foreign and international terms officially adopted in Italian, as well.

The consonants b, f, m, n, v are pronounced as in English. The approximate English equivalents are as follows:

B Always as an English b. Example:
Bene » well.
Bambino » Child
F Always as an English f in fame, knife, flute, but never as in of. Example:
Fare » To make
Famoso » famous
H is completely soundless; never as in house, hope, hammer; but as in heir, honest. H is written in some form of the verb avere to have, in few other Italian words, and mainly in foreign words and names. Examples:
Ho » (I) have.
Hai » (you) have.
Ha » (he / she / it) has.
Hanno » (they) have.
Ahi! » (interj) ouch!.
Hotel » hotel.
L is sharper and more forward in the mouth than in English, similar to l in link. Examples:
Olio » oil
Lingua » language
Sale » salt
Lungo » long
Melone » melon
Luna » moon
Scuola » school
M Always as an English m. Examples:
Madre » Mother
N Always as an English n. Examples:
No » No
Nonna » Grandmother
P is as in English, but without the aspiration that sometimes accompanies this sound in English. Examples:
Pane » bread
Patata » potato
Pepe » pepper
Papà » dad
Popone » melon

Ponte » bridge

T is approximately the same as in English, but no escaping of breath accompanies it in Italian. Examples:
Contento » glad
Carta » paper
Arte » art
Matita » pencil
Turista » tourist
Antipasto » appetizer
Telefono » telephone
Testa » head
V Always as an English v. Examples:
Vino » Wine.
Voglio » (I) want.

DIFFICULT CONSONANTS

Some consonants have two pronunciations, depending on the letter (generally a vowel) that is before that consonant.

Also INDICAR QUE TAMBIEN EXSITEN LOS CLUSTER, LAS DOBLES CONSONANTES Y OTROS

- » [Consonantic Digraphs](#)
- » [Special clusters in Italian Language](#)
- » [Double Consonants in Italian Language](#)

The approximate English equivalents for these consonants are as follows:

c-C: This consonant has two pronunciations:
When "c" is followed by "a", "o", "u" or any consonant you pronounce it as in the English word Cat. It sounds like the English k. Example:
Casa » house.
Credere v to think, believe.
Con » with.
Colesseo » Colosseum.
Capo » head.
Cupido » Cupid.
Cane » dog.

Camera » camera.
Caffè » coffee.
When "c" is followed by "e" or "i" you pronounce it as you do the first and last sound in the English word Church, or like the English sound ch in chest. Examples:
Cena » supper.
Voce » voice.
Cibo » food.
Concerto » concert.
Aceto » vinegar.
Cinema » cinema
Cipolla » onion.
d-D: This consonant is somewhat more explosive than in English, with the tongue near the tip of the upper teeth but with no aspiration. Examples:
Di » of.
Dove » where.
Due » two.
Denaro » money.
Dodici » twelve.
Donna » woman.
Lunedì » Monday.
Moda » fashion.
Undici » eleven.
g-G: This consonant has two pronunciations:
When g is followed by "a", "o", "u", or any consonant, you pronounce it as you pronounce the g in the English word "good", or like "go". Examples:
Albergo » hotel.
Gamba » leg.
Gusto » taste.
Fungo » mushroom.
Gonna » skirt.
Gomma » eraser.
Lungo » long.
Guanti » gloves.
Guidare » to drive.
Lingua » tongue.
When g is followed by "e" or "i", you pronounce it as you do the first sound in the English word job or like the "g" in gem. Examples:
Gelato » ice cream.
Angelo » angel.
Pagina » page.
Gente » people.

Gesso » chalk.
Gentile » kind.
Gita » outing.
Gennaio » January.

Some consonants have two pronunciations, depending on the letter (generally a vowel) that is before that consonant.

The approximate English equivalents for these consonants are as follows:

q-Q: This consonant exists only in connection with u followed by another vowel; that is, you always find qu. The "q" is pronounced like (k), or like the English "qu" in quest. Examples:
Questo » this.
Quinto » fifth.
Quale » which.
Quarto » fourth.
Quanto » how much.
Quantità » quantity.
Quadro » picture.
Qualità » quality.

r-R: This sound is always "rolled", like a Scottish "r" in Edinburgh, or a Spanish "r" in señor. You don't pronounce the Italian r with your tongue in the back, as you do the English r; rather, you can obtain this sound making the tip of the tongue vibrate almost against the hard palate, next to the back of the upper teeth. It never sounds as an English r, nor as a French r. Examples:
Ora » now.
Tenore » tenor.
Albergo » hotel.
Baritono » baritone.
Arte » art.
Orologio » watch.
Porta » door.
Sardina » sardine.

s-S: This consonant has two pronunciations:
S is sometimes strong and hissing like the English "s" in house, set, strip. Example:
Soggiorno » living room.
Testa » head.
Stanza » room.
Festa » party; holiday.

Posta » mail.
Stufato » stew.
Pasta » pasta; dough; pastry.
Pista » track.
S is sometimes (but always before b, d, g, l, m, n, r, and v) like the english s in easy, or the the English "z" in zoo. Examples:
Rosa » rose.
Casa » house.
Tesoro » treasure.
Frase » phrase.
Sbaglio » mistake.
Esercizio » exercise.
Svelto » quick.
Musica » music.
Sgridare » to scold.
Sbadato » careless.
z-Z: This consonant has two pronunciations(*):
Z is sometimes voiceless, like ts is bets, cats. Example:
Pizza » pizza.
Negozio » store.
Marzo » March.
Venezia » Venice.
Grazie » thank you.
Dizionario » dictionary.
Z is sometimes voiced, like ds in beds. Examples:
Zero » zero.
Zebra » zebra.
Pranzo » lunch.
Zelo » zeal.
Romanzo » novel.
Zanzara » mosquito.

(*) In either case, its sound differs more distinctly from s than it does in English.

STRESS & ACCENT MARKS

Stress is the audible accent that you put on a syllable as you speak it. One syllable always gets more stress than all the others. Although there is no strict rule, in most Italian words the accent or stress falls on penultimate syllable. But for this rule there are too many exceptions.

In Italian, only vowels have accents. All vowels at the end of a word can have this accent (`), but only the "e" can have both (`) and (´). The difference lies only in the pronunciation. That is, è is pronounced very open, as in "hell", whereas é is more closed, as in "gourmet". Here are some examples:

Caffè ("kahf-feh") » coffee

Città ("cheet-tah") » city

Lunedì ("loo-neh-dee") » Monday

Perché ("pehr-keh") » why; because

Però ("peh-roh") » but

Università ("oo-nee-vehr-see-tah") » university

Virtù ("veer-too") » virtue

Is very unusual for Italian words to be spelt with accented letters, with very few exceptions discussed further in this page.

In ordinary spelling accented vowels are allowed, but very seldom used. Only in two cases accented vowels are commonly used:

Words whose last syllable carries the accent:

There are many words of this kind in Italian (nouns, verb inflections, adverbs, etc.), and some are frequently used. An accent is compulsory in this case, otherwise the stress would not be heard. Furthermore, in some cases the same word spelt without an accent even has a different meaning (see further down). A few words with a similar spelling, but whose last syllable is not stressed, are shown on the right:

Perché » why, because
Sarà » it will be (*Sara* » Sarah, a name)
Perciò » therefore
Papà » dad (*Papa* » pope)
Però » but, however (*Pero* » pear-tree)
Farò » I'll do (*Faro* » light-house)
Più » more, plus

Also several compounds of che (pronounced "ke", meaning which, that) are spelt with an accent:
Perché » why, because
Poiché » because
Benché » despite
Giacché » since
Sicché » so, therefore etc.

Words that have a different meaning depending on the position of the accent:

A few words have a different meaning when different syllables carry the accent. Note that the stress is in the underlined syllable:
àncora "**ahn**kohrah" » anchor (noun)
ancòra "ahn**koh**rah" » again, more (adverb)
règia "**reh**jah" » royal (adjective)
regìa "reh**jy**hah" » direction of a movie or a play (noun)
capitàno "kahpy**tah**noh" » captain (noun)
càpitano "**kah**pytahnoh" » they happen, they occur (verb)
làvati "**lah**vahtih" » wash yourself
lavàti "lah**vah**tih" » masculine plural of washed

In this case, accents are not mandatory; in most cases they are not used, therefore the correct pronunciation of the word is understood only by the context of the phrase: for instance, considering the third couple of sample words, in sentences such as "sometimes strange things happen" or "he is the captain of the ship", neither of the two words could be mistaken with the other.

III. Tenses

Verbs are fundamental to any language, and Italian is no exception. There are three primary groups of Italian verbs, classified according to the ending of their infinitives: first conjugation (-*are* verbs), second conjugation (-*ere* verbs), and third conjugation(-*ire* verbs). Most Italian verbs belong to the first-conjugation group and follow a highly uniform pattern. Once you learn how to conjugate one -*are* verb, you've essentially learned hundreds of them. And what about those Italian verbs that don't end in -*are*? Second-conjugation (-*ere*) verbs account for approximately one-quarter of all Italian verbs. Although many have some sort of irregular structure, there are also many regular -*ere*verbs. The final group of Italian verbs is those that end in -*ire*.

Feeling Tense? A Little Moody?

Feeling tense studying Italian verbs? Or maybe you're a bit moody. There *is* a difference. Mood (a variation of the word "mode") refers to the attitude of the speaker toward what he or she is saying. There are four finite moods (*modi finiti*) in Italian: indicative (*indicativo*), which is used to indicate facts; subjunctive (*congiuntivo*), which is used to express an attitude or feeling toward an event; conditional(*condizionale*), which is used to express what would happen in a hypothetical situation; and imperative (*imperativo*), which is used to give commands. (Note that modern English only has three finite moods: indicative, subjunctive, and imperative.)

There are also three indefinite moods (*modi indefiniti*) in Italian, so-called because the forms do not indicate the person (i.e., first, second, or third): infinitive (*infinito*), participle (*participio*), and gerund (*gerundio*).

Moods are divided into one or more tenses, which indicates the time when the action of the verb takes place (present, past, or future). For reference, the chart below lists the mood and tenses of Italian verbs in English and Italian.

ITALIAN VERBS: MOOD AND TENSE

Indicative / Indicativo
present / presente
present perfect / passato prossimo
imperfect / imperfetto
past perfect / trapassato prossimo
absolute past / passato remoto
preterite perfect / trapassato remoto
future / futuro semplice
future perfect / futuro anteriore

Subjunctive / Congiuntivo
present / presente
past / passato
imperfect / imperfetto
past perfect / trapassato

Conditional / **Condizionale**
present / presente
past / passato

Imperative / **Imperativo**
present / presente

Infinitive / Infinitivo
present / presente
past / passato

Participle / Participio
present / presente
past / passato
Gerund / Gerundio
present / presente
past / passato
Conjugating Italian Verbs
Singular
I person
II person
III person
Plural
I person
II person
III person

Learning six forms for every verb would be an endless task. Fortunately, most Italian verbs are regular verbs, meaning they are conjugated following a regular pattern. In fact, there are only three irregular first conjugation verbs. Once the regular verb endings are memorized the pattern can be applied to other verbs of the same group. Or, they are irregular, and do not follow a regular pattern.

Although numerous, even the irregular second and third conjugation verbs fall into a few groups that make it easier to memorize.

Essere and Avere: Don't Leave Home Without Them

Language means action, and you can't speak Italian without the verbs essere (to be) and avere (to have). These two essential verbs are used in compound verb formations, idiomatic expressions, and many other grammatical constructions. Become the *maestro* of these two verbs and you'll have taken a giant step towards learning Italian.

In Transit

Ready for action? Then it's time for a transitive verb—those that take a direct object(*complemento oggetto*): *Luisa legge un libro* (Luisa reads a book). Transitive verbs can also be used in the absolute sense; that is, with an implicit direct object: *Luisa legge* (Luisa reads [a book, magazine, newspaper]). Intransitive verbs, on the other hand, are those that never take a direct object: Giorgio *cammina* (Giorgio walks). Some verbs can be classified as either transitive or intransitive, depending on the context of the sentence.

Verbs with Voice!

Italian verbs (like verbs in many other languages) have two voices. A verb is in the active voice when the subject carries out or performs the action of the verb: *Marco ha preparato le valigie* (Marco packed the suitcases). A verb is in the passive voice when the subject is acted on by the verb: *La scena è stata filmata da un famoso regista* (The scene was filmed by a famous director). Only transitive verbs with an explicit direct object can be transformed from the active voice to the passive voice.

Mirror, Mirror, on the Wall

You wake up (*svegliarsi*), take a shower (*farsi la doccia*), comb your hair (*pettinarsi*), and get dressed (*vestirsi*). You couldn't start your day without reflexive verbs (*verbi riflessivi*). Those are verbs whose action reverts to the subject: *Mi lavo* (I wash myself). In Italian, reflexive pronouns (*i pronomi reflessivi*) are required when conjugating reflexive verbs.

Coulda, Woulda, Shoulda

There are three important Italian verbs known as *verbi servili* or *verbi modali* (modal verbs). These verbs, *potere* (to be able to, can), *volere* (to want), *dovere* (to have to, must), can stand alone, taking on their given meaning. They can also follow the infinitive of other verbs, functioning to modify the meaning of those verbs.

Verbs That End In -*sene*, -*sela*, -*cela*

There are a group of Italian verbs that are conjugated with two different pronoun particles. Verbs such as *meravigliarsene* and *provarcisi* are called pronominal verbs(*verbi pronominali*). In fact, they are still classified as either first-conjugation (-*are*verbs), second-conjugation (-*ere* verbs), or third-conjugation (-*ire* verbs) according to the ending of their infinitives. Many pronominal verbs are used idiomatically.

Shadowed By A Preposition

Certain Italian verbs (and expressions) are followed by specific prepositions such as *a*, *di*, *per*, and *su*. But to the consternation of students of all levels and abilities, there is no hard-and-fast set of rules governing this grammatical usage. This is one instance in which language learners must familiarize themselves with tables that include Italian verbs and expressions followed by specific prepositions as well as verbs followed directly by the infinitive.

Present Perfect Tense

The *passato prossimo*—grammatically referred to as the present perfect— expresses a fact or action that happened in the recent past or that occurred long ago but still has ties to the present.

It's a compound tense (*tempo composto*), which means that you need to use an auxiliary verb — either "*essere*" or "*avere*" — plus a past participle. An example of a past participle would be "*mangiato*" for the verb "*mangiare*".

If you want to talk about events that happened repeatedly in the past, like going to your Italian lesson every Sunday, or telling a story, you'll need to use the imperfect tense.

Here Are a Few Examples of How the *Passato Prossimo* Appears in Italian:

Ti ho appena chiamato. - I just called you.

Mi sono iscritto/a all'università quattro anni fa. - I entered university four years ago.

Questa mattina sono uscito/a presto. - This morning I left early.

Il Petrarca ha scritto sonetti immortali. - Petrarca wrote enduring sonnets.

How to Form the Past Tense

In order to form the past tense, there are two main things you need to know.
Does the verb you want to use need the auxiliary verb "*essere*" or "*avere*"?
What is the past participle of the verb you want to use?
For example, if you wanted to say, "I went to Rome last summer", you would need to use the verb "*andare*". The verb "*andare*" takes the verb "*essere*" as a helper, or auxiliary, verb because it's a verb that has to do with motion. Then, the past participle of the verb "*andare*" is "*andato*". However, when you use the verb "*essere*" as an auxiliary verb, the past participle MUST agree in number and gender.

Ad esempio:

L'estate scorsa sono andato a Roma. - I went to Rome last summer. (masculine, singular)
L'estate scorsa sono andata a Roma. - I went to Rome last summer. (feminine, singular)
L'estate scorsa mia sorella e mia madre sono andate a Roma. - My sister and mother went to Rome last summer. (feminine, plural)
L'estate scorsa siamo andati a Roma. - We went to Rome last summer. (masculine, plural)

If you're using "*avere*" as an auxiliary verb, it's much simpler as the past participle does not have to agree in number and gender (that is, unless you're using direct object pronouns.)
For example, let's use the sentence, "I watched that movie".
First, you need to use the verb "*guardare* - to watch". The past participle of "*guardare*" is "*guardato*". Then you conjugate your auxiliary verb "*avere*" into the first person singular, which is "*ho*".
The sentence then becomes, "*Ho guardato quel film*".

TIP: If the verb you're using is reflexive, like "*innamorarsi* - to fall in love", you need to use "*essere*" as your auxiliary verb. For example, "*Ci siamo innamorati due anni fa.* - We fell in love two years ago."

When to Use Il Passato Prossimo (Present Perfect) Instead of L'Imperfetto (Imperfect)

It is notoriously difficult to correctly decide between *il passato prossimo* and *l'imperfetto* when you try talking about the past in Italian. While there are some rules for when to choose one or the other, it's also helpful to know which phrases are typically used with *il passato prossimo*.
The following table lists some adverbial expressions that are often used with the *passato prossimo*:

Common Expressions Used with Il Passato Prossimo

ieri	yesterday

ieri pomeriggio	yesterday afternoon
ieri sera	last night
il mese scorso	last month
l'altro giorno	the other day
stamattina	this morning
tre giorni fa	three days ago

Italian imperfect Tense

How do you express that sentiment in Italian? It's something that happened in the past, but since it was something that happened often, you wouldn't use the present perfect, or il passato prossimo.

In this and similar cases, which we'll discuss throughout this article, you would use the imperfect tense.

Lucky for you, this tense, l'*imperfetto,* is formed by adding the same endings to all three conjugations. The only difference is the typical vowel of the infinitive.

What's more, you should know that the imperfect tense is much more frequently used in Italian than in English. It expresses the English "used to" and is used to describe actions or conditions that lasted an indefinite time in the past. It's also used to express a habitual action in the past and to describe time, age, and weather in the past. So if you like telling stories, it's a critical tense to learn.

Adverbial Expressions That Are Commonly Used with the Imperfect Tense:

a volte - at times, sometimes
continuamente - continuously
giorno dopo giorno - day in and day out
ogni tanto - once in awhile
sempre - always
spesso spesso - again and again
tutti i giorni - every day

How to Conjugate Regular Verbs in the Imperfect Tense

Mangiare - To eat (regular verbs with -are endings)

Mangiavo - I ate	Mangiavamo - We ate
Mangiavi - You ate	Mangiavate - You (all) ate

Mangiava - He/she/it ate	Mangiavano - They ate

<u>Finire</u> - To finish (regular verbs with -ire endings)

Finivo - I finished	Finivamo - We finished
Finivi - You finished	Finivate - You (all) finished
Finiva - He/she/it finished	Finivano - They finished

<u>Prendere</u> - To take, to get (regular verbs with -ere endings)

Prendevo - I took	Prendevamo - We took
Prendevi - You took	Prendevate - You (all) took
Prendeva - He/she/it took	Prendevano - They took

Using Common, Irregular Verbs

<u>Essere</u> - To be

Ero - I was	Eravamo - We were
Eri - You were	Eravate - You (all) were
Era - He/she/it was	Erano - They were

<u>Fare</u> - To do/to make

Facevo - I did	Facevamo - We did
Facevi - You did	Facevate - You (all) did
Faceva - He/she/it did	Facevano - They did

<u>Dire</u> - To say, to tell

Dicevo - I said	Dicevamo - We said
Dicevi - You said	Dicevate - You (all) said
Diceva - He/she/it said	Dicevano - They said

Examples Using L'*imperfetto*:

Ogni domenica, quando ero un bambino/a, mia nonna ci preparava una splendida cena. Every Sunday, when I was a kid, my nonna cooked us a big dinner.

Giocavo a calcio ogni pomeriggio. I played soccer every afternoon.

Quando ero piccolo/a, mangiavo la pasta ogni giorno. When I was a kid, I ate pasta every day.

La settimana scorsa, era (c'era) un tempo bellissimo! Last week, it was really beautiful weather!

Loro credevano sempre a tutto. They always believed everything.
Volevamo andare in Italia. We wanted to go to Italy.
Il cielo era sempre blu. The sky was always blue.

Ogni mattina, prendevo un bel cappuccino e un cornetto vuoto. Every morning, I got a cappuccino and a plain croissant.

Nel 2000, avevo quarant'anni. In 2000, I was forty years old.
Mi ricordo quello che diceva sempre mio padre: "Guarda il ceppo"! I remember what my dad always used to say: "Take a look at the log"! (figurative = the family)

Italian Past Perfect Tense

In English, the past perfect tense (*trapassato prossimo*) is formed with the auxiliary "had" plus the past participle of the main verb. In Italian, the *trapassato prossimo*, a compound tense, is formed with the imperfetto of the auxiliary verb avere or essereand the past participle of the acting verb.

The students were tired because they had studied until late. He didn't go to the theater because he had already seen the film. The past perfect tense (*trapassato prossimo*) is used when two actions happened at different times in the past.

Here are a few examples of the *trapassato prossimo*:

Già erano partiti quando sono arrivato. (They had already left when I arrived.)
Avevo chiuso le finestre quando è cominciato a piovere. (I had shut the windows when it started to rain.)
La macchina sbandava perché aveva piovuto. (The car was sliding because it had rained.)

Using Auxiliary Verb Avere

The appropriate tense of *avere* or *essere* (called the auxiliary or helping verbs) and the past participle of the target verb forms the verb phrase.

Avere is used in a myriad of grammatical and linguistic situations. Learning the many conjugations and uses of the verb is crucial to the study of the Italian language.

In general, transitive verbs are conjugated with avere. Transitive verbs express an action that carries over from the subject to the direct object: *The teacher explains the lesson.*

The past participle is invariable when the passato prossimo is constructed with avere. Today Anna isn't working because she worked yesterday. *Oggi Anna non lavora perchè ha lavorato ieri.*

The others worked yesterday too. *Anche gli altri hanno lavorato ieri.*

When the past participle of a verb conjugated with avere is preceded by the third person <u>direct object pronouns</u> **lo, la, le,** or **li,** the past participle agrees with the preceding direct object pronoun in gender and number.

Avere is an irregular verb (un verbo irregolare); it does not follow a predictable pattern of conjugation.

Using Auxiliary Verb Essere

When using *essere*, the past participle always agrees in gender and number with the subject of the verb. It can therefore have four endings: **-o, -a, -i, -e**. In many cases, intransitive verbs (those that cannot take a direct object), especially those expressing motion, are conjugated with the auxiliary verb *essere*.

The verb *essere* is also conjugated with itself as the auxiliary verb.

Some of the most common verbs that form compound tenses with *essere* include:

andare — to go
arrivare — to arrive
cadere — to fall, to drop
costare — to cost
crescere — to grow
diventare — to become
durare — to last, to continue
entrare — to enter
morire — to die
nascere — to be born
partire — to leave, to depart
restare — to stay, to remain
tornare — to return
uscire — to exit
venire — to come

Conjugating Italian Verbs in the Past Perfect with Avere and Essere

	PARLARE	*CREDERE*	*ANDARE*	*USCIRE*
io	*avevo parlato*	*avevo creduto*	*ero andato(-a)*	*ero uscito(-a)*
tu	*avevi parlato*	*avevi creduto*	*eri andato(-a)*	*eri uscito(-a)*
lui, lei, Lei	*aveva parlato*	*aveva creduto*	*era andato(-a)*	*era uscito(-a)*
noi	*avevamo parlato*	*avevamo creduto*	*eravamo andati(-e)*	*eravamo usciti(-e)*
voi	*avevate parlato*	*avevate creduto*	*eravate andati(-e)*	*eravate usciti(-e)*

loro, Loro	avevano parlato	avevano creduto	erano andati(-e)	erano usciti(-e)

Remote Past Tense

The remote past tense (*passato remoto*), although typically used to talk about history or in literature, is actually a simple tense and is formed by one word.

In general, as we referenced, it refers to the historical past or to events that have happened in the distant past relative to the speaker.

However, there are many places in the south of Italy that still use the remote past tense as the *passato prossimo*. For example, someone might use the past remote tense to talk about something that happened just two weeks ago.

How to Form the Past Remote Tense

Follow this format to form the *passato remoto* of regular verbs:

For -are verbs, drop the infinitive ending and add one of these personal endings to the root: *-ai, -asti, -ò, -ammo, -aste, -arono*.

For -ere verbs, drop the infinitive ending and add these personal endings to the root: *-ei, -esti, -é, -emmo, -este, -erono*. Note that many regular -ere verbs have an alternative form in the first person singular, third person singular, and third person plural forms.

For -ire verbs, drop the infinitive ending and add these personal endings to the root: *-ii, -isti, -í, -immo, -iste, -irono*.

Here are a few examples of how the remote past is used in Italian:

Dante si rifugiò a Ravenna. - Dante took refuge in Ravenna.
Petrarca morì nel 1374. - Petrarca died in 1374.
Michelangelo nacque nel 1475. - Michelangelo was born in 1475.

The table below provides examples of three regular Italian verbs (one of each class) conjugated in the remote past tense.

Conjugating Italian Verbs in the Remote Past Tense

	PARLARE	RICEVERE	CAPIRE
io	*parlai*	*ricevei (ricevetti)*	*capii*
tu	*parlasti*	*ricevesti*	*capisti*
lui, lei, Lei	*parlò*	*ricevé (ricevette)*	*capí*
noi	*parlammo*	*ricevemmo*	*capimmo*

voi	*parlaste*	*riceveste*	*capiste*
loro, Loro	*parlarono*	*riceverono (ricevettero)*	*capirono*

Irregular Verbs in the Past Remote Tense

Like with most verbs in Italian, there are plenty of irregular ones in the past remote tense. Here are five common verbs.

1) Essere – To be

fui fummo
fosti foste
fu furono

— **Albert Einstein fu un uomo di grande saggezza.** – Albert Einstein was a man of great wisdom.

— **"Fatti non foste per viver come bruti..."** - "Consider your origins: You were not born to live like brutes." [Dante, La Divina Commedia, canto XXVI)

2) Avere – To have

ebbi avemmo
avesti aveste
ebbe ebbero

— **Ebbero così tanta fortuna da vincere persino il primo premio della lotteria nazionale!** - They had such luck that they also won the first prize of the National Lottery!

— **Giulia ebbe il coraggio di donare un rene a sua sorella.** - Giulia had the courage to donate a kidney to her sister.

3) Fare – To do/make

feci facemmo
facesti faceste
fece fecero

— **Con pochi soldi fecero un matrimonio bellissimo.** – They set up a beautiful wedding with little money.

— **Facemmo tutto il possibile per riportare alla luce l'affresco di Raffaello.** - We did everything possible to bring to light Raffaello's fresco.

4) Stare – To stay/to be

stetti stemmo
stesti steste
stette stettero

— **Mi ricordo che stetti in silenzio tutta la festa. Ero troppo timida!** - I remember I spent the whole party without saying a word. I was too shy!

— **I feriti, dopo la scoperta della penicillina nel 1937, stettero subito meglio.** - The wounded felt immediately better after the discovery of penicillin in 1937.

5) <u>Dire</u> – **To say**

dissi dicemmo
dicesti diceste
disse dissero

— **Cimabue disse: "L'allievo ha superato il maestro."** – Cimabue said: "The pupil has surpassed the teacher."

— **Romeo e Giulietta si dissero parole d'amore che sono arrivate fino ai nostri tempi!** - Romeo and Juliet said words of love to each other that have persisted until the present!

Italian Preterite Perfect Tense

You've learned about the passato remoto tense, which is the one you use in literature or to talk about events that happened in history. But you have also learned the trapassato remoto tense?

As you'll see below, it's a tense for students who are more advanced in their studies.

It's used primarily in literary contexts and is known in English as the preterite perfect. It's a <u>compound tense</u> formed with the <u>passato remoto</u> of the auxiliary verb <u>avere</u> or <u>essere</u> and the <u>past participle</u> of the acting verb.

For example, a sentence like the one below, in a literary context, would require the trapassato remoto.

As soon as Julia had gone down the stairs, she left the building. - Dopo che Giulia ebbe sceso le scale, uscì dal palazzo.

"Ebbe sceso" comes from the conjugated verb "essere - to be" and "sceso" is the past participle of the verb "scendere - to go down."

The action indicated by the verb *scendere* (to descend—conjugated in the past perfect) occurs prior to the action indicated by the verb *uscire* (to exit, to leave—conjugated in the <u>passato remoto</u>).

The past perfect is a verb form that is used to refer to events, experiences, or facts that happened or were already completed before a point of reference in the past.

In each sentence set in the *trapassato remoto*, you will encounter an expression of time, such as the following: *appena* (barely), *dopo che* (as soon as), or *finché non* (up until).

For example:

- **Partirono, quando ebbero ricevuto la notizia.** - They were leaving when they received the notice.
- **Renata entrò, appena Giorgio fu uscito.** - Renata entered just after Giorgio had left.
- **Andò a casa, quando ebbe finito di lavorare.** - He went home when he had finished working.
- **Dopo che ebbe letto quel libro, lei ne comprò uno nuovo.** - After she had read that book, she bought a new one.
- **Non appena ebbi iniziato a guidare, ebbi bisogno di usare il bagno.** - As soon as I started driving, I had to use the bathroom.

Most verbs of the second conjugation are irregular in the *passato remoto* tense.

To see how *avere* and *essere* are conjugated in the remote past tense, see the table below.

TRAPASSATO REMOTO OF THE VERB AVERE

Person	Singular	Plural
I	(io) ebbi	(noi) avemmo
II	(tu) avesti	(voi) aveste
III	(lui, lei, Lei) ebbe	(loro, Loro) ebbero

TRAPASSATO REMOTO OF THE VERB ESSERE

Person	Singular	Plural
I	(io) fui	(noi) fummo
II	(tu) fosti	(voi) foste
III	(lui, lei, Lei) fu	(loro, Loro) furono

Note that if the verb requires "essere," then you must change the ending of the past participle to agree with the subject in gender and number.

For example: Dopo che le ragazze furono salite sull'autobus, si sedettero. - After the girls got on the bus, they sat down.

Italian Future Indicative Tense

The future shows a simple fact that has yet to occur or come to fruition:

Arriverò domani.

Terminerò il lavoro entro una settimana.

The future can take value imperative:

Farete esattamente come vi ho detto.
Imparerai questa poesia a memoria.

	BRANDIRE	**GUSTARE**	**RIDURRE**	**VINIFICARE**
io	brandirò	gusterò	ridurrò	vinificerò
tu	brandirai	gusterai	ridurrai	vinificerai
lui, lei, Lei	brandirà	gusterà	ridurrà	vinificerà
noi	brandiremo	gusteremo	ridurremo	vinificeremo
voi	brandirete	gusterete	ridurrete	vinificerete
loro, Loro	brandiranno	gusteranno	ridurranno	vinificeranno

CONJUGATING ITALIAN VERBS IN THE PRETERITE PERFECT INDICATIVE TENSE
Word formation in Italian is the linguistic process (think vocabulary building) in which terms can be transformed from base words to **suffissati** (suffixed words)—*orologio » orologiaio*, **prefissati** (prefixed words)—*campionato » precampionato*, and **composti** (compounds)—*fermare + carte » fermacarte*.

The formation of words enriches the Italian language from within. In fact, it produces new vocabulary—as in *orologiaio* (watchmaker), *precampionato* (preseason), *fermacarte* (paperweight)—starting with vocabulary that already exists—in this case, *orologio* (watch), *campionato* (season), *fermare* (to hold, detain, secure), and *carte* (paper).

The **suffisso** (suffix) is the particle that appears at the end of the suffixed, for example -**aio** in *orologiaio*. The **prefisso** (prefix) is instead the particle that appears at the beginning of the prefixed, for example **pre-** in *precampionato*. Together, the suffixes and prefixes are known as affixes; the suffix -**aio** in *orologiaio* and the prefix **pre-** in *precampionato* are, therefore, two affixes.

Composti (compounds) are formed by the merger into a single word of at least two words; this is the case of *fermare* and *carte* in the compound word *fermacarte*.

All Italian speakers can construct, starting from certain **basi** (bases) and making the necessary modifications, a whole series of new words (the technical term is defined as **neoformazione**—a compound or derivative recently introduced to the language). So, for example, *orologiaio*, *precampionato*, and *fermacarte* are new words derived from *orologio*, *campionato*, *fermare*, and *carte*. To go from the base to the new term there are certain rules of transformation.

Word Formation Is Not Simple Addition

The formation of words does not consist in the mere addition of elements: base + suffix = suffixed; prefix + base = prefixed; word + word = compound word. This, in fact, it is only the appearance of the phenomenon. The formation of words instead assumes that the speaker has is fully aware of the meaning of the relationship linking the new word to its base. For example, everyone (or at least native Italian speakers) will recognize in words such as *scaffalature* and *librone* a connection to *scaffale* and *libro*, but nobody will think that *struttura* and *mattone* are linked to *strutto* and *matto*. Only in the first case can an equivalence be formulated:

insieme di scaffali has the same meaning as *scaffalatura* (shelf unit)
grosso libro has the same meaning as *librone* (big book, tome)
While in the second case:
insieme di strutto (lard as a whole) has a different meaning than *struttura* (structure)
grosso matto (big madman) has a different meaning than *mattone* (brick)

As shown, the formation of words in Italian cannot be explained only by taking into consideration the formal relationship that links a base with an affix (*-ura*, *-one*, and others); it is also necessary to consider the relationship between the meanings. The formation of words can be divided into three categories: **suffissazione** (suffixation), **prefissazione** (prefixation), and **composizione** (composition).

Italian Future Perfect Tense

"In two years, I will have learned Italian."

How do you express a sentence like that in Italian? You use a tense called *il futuro anteriore*, or the future perfect tense in English.

You'll notice that it looks similar to the *il futuro semplice*, the simple future tense, but has an extra addition.

Here's what that sentence above will look like: *Fra due anni, sarò riuscito/a ad imparare l'italiano.*

If you're familiar with the future tense, you'll notice the "*sarò*", which is the first person conjugation of the verb "*essere* - to be". Immediately after, you'll see another verb "*riuscire* - to succeed at/to be able to" in a past participle form.

(If you're not sure a past participle is, take a look at this article. It's basically just the form a verb changes to when you need to talk about something that happened in the past. Other examples you might recognize are "*mangiato*" for the verb "*mangiare*" and "*vissuto*" for the verb "*vivere*".)

I'll give you a few examples first and then we'll break down how you can start forming and using the *futuro anteriore*.

Esempi

- **Alle sette avremo già mangiato.** - By seven we'll already have eaten.
- **Noi avremo parlato al padre di Anna.** - We will already have spoken to Anna's father.
- **Marco non è venuto alla festa, sarà stato molto impegnato.** - Marco didn't come to the party, he must have been very busy.

When to Use It

Typically you'll use this verb tense when you're talking about an action in the future (like you having already eaten) before something else happens (like it being 7 PM).

You can also use it when you're unsure about something that's happening in the future or that happened in the past, like you thinking that the reason Marco didn't come to the party was because he was busy. In this case, other words that you could use instead of forming the futuro anteriore would be "*forse* - maybe", "*magari* - maybe" or "*probabilmente* - probably".

How to Form the Futuro Anteriore

As you saw above, the *futuro anteriore* is created when you combine a future tense conjugation (like *sarò*) with a past participle (like *riuscito*), which makes it a compound tense. To be more specific though (and easier on you), there are only two verbs that you can use in the future tense conjugation spot, and they are the auxiliary verbs avere or essere.

Take a look at the two tables below that show you the future tense conjugations for the verbs "*essere* - to be" and "*avere* - to have".

Essere - To Be

Sarò - I will be	Saremo - We will be

Sarai - You will be	Sarete - You all will be
Sarà - He/she/it will be	Saranno - They will be

Avere - To Have

Avrò - I will have	Avremo - We will have
Avrai - You will have	Avrete - You all will have
Avrà - He/she/it will have	Avranno - They will have

How Do You Choose Between "Essere" and "Avere"?|

When you're deciding which auxiliary verb to use -- either "*essere*" or "*avere*" -- you use the same logic as you would when you're choosing "*essere*" or "*avere*" with the passato prossimo tense. So, as a quick reminder, reflexive verbs, like "*sedersi - to sit oneself*", and most verbs that are related to mobility, like "*andare - to go*", "*uscire - to go out*", or "*partire - to leave*", will be paired with "*essere*". Most other verbs, like "*mangiare - to eat*", "*usare - to use*", and "*vedere - to look*", will be paired with "*avere*".

Andare - To Go

Sarò andato/a - I will have gone	Saremo andati/e - We will have gone
Sarai andato/a - You will have gone	Sarete andati/e - You (all) will have gone
Sarà andato/a - He/she/it will have gone	Saranno andati/e - They will have gone

Mangiare - To Eat

Avrò mangiato - I will have eaten	Avremo mangiato - We will have eaten
Avrai mangiato - You will have eaten	Avrete mangiato - You (all) will have eaten
Avrà mangiato - He/she/it will have eaten	Avranno mangiato - They will have eaten

Esempi

Quando avrò finito questo piatto, verrò da te. - When I will have finished this dish, I will go to your place.

Sarai stata felicissima quando hai ottenuto la promozione! - You must have been/I imagine you were happy when you got the promotion!

Appena avrò guardato questo film, te lo darò. - As soon as I have watched this movie, I will give it to you.

Riuscirai a parlare l'italiano fluentemente quando avrai fatto molta pratica. - You will succeed at speaking Italian fluently when you will have practiced it a lot.

Appena ci saremo sposati, compreremo una casa. - As soon as we are married, we will buy a house.

Section (B): Basic Vocabulary for Travelers

Italian Greetings

Knowing Italian greetings can make a good impression, whether you're speaking Italian for business or while traveling. The Italian culture places importance on introductions and salutations as it is often considered a foundational way of showing respect. There are different expressions you can use depending on if the situation is formal (business meeting) or informal (meeting someone at a restaurant). Offer polite greetings to friends and associates or as a way to break the ice when meeting new people.
Practice using these common Italian greetings:
Buongiorno! (bwohn-*johr*-noh) (Hello! and Good morning!)
Arrivederci! (*ahr*-ree-veh-*dehr*-chee) (Goodbye!) (Formal)
Ciao! (chou) (Hello! and Good-bye!) (Informal)
Salve! (*sahl*-veh) (Hello! and Good-bye!) (Neutral)
Buonasera! (*bwoh*-nah-*seh*-rah) (Good afternoon! Good evening!) (Formal)
Buonanotte! (*bwoh*-nah-*noht*-teh) (Good night!) (Informal)
Come si chiama? (*koh*-meh see *kyah*-mah) (What is your name?) (Formal)
Come ti chiami? (*koh*-meh tee *kyah*-mee) (What is your name?) (Informal)
Mi chiamo… (mee *kyah*-moh) (My name is. . .)
Come sta? (*koh*-meh stah) (How are you?) (Formal)
Come stai? (*koh*-meh stahy) (How are you?) (Informal)
Bene, grazie. (*beh*-neh *grah*-tsee-eh) (Fine, thank you.)
Italian Courtesy Phrases
Courtesy is important no matter what country you're in. Use these courtesy phrases when speaking in Italian so you can be considerate and polite; they'll also help you communicate easily:
Per favore (pehr fah-*voh*-reh) (Please.)
Per piacere (pehr pyah-*cheh*-reh) (Please.)
Grazie (*grah*-tsee-eh) (Thank you.)
Prego! (*preh*-goh) (You're welcome!; By all means, after you.)
Non c'è di che. (nohn cheh dee keh) (You're welcome.)
Mi dispiace. (mee dees-*pyah*-cheh) (I'm sorry.)
Mi scusi. (mee *skooh*-zee) (Excuse me, formal.)

Scusi, un informazione, per favore. (*skooh*-zee oohn-*een*-fohr-mats-*yoh*-neh pehr fah-*voh*-reh) (Excuse me, I need some information, please.)

Scusa. (*skooh*-zah) (Excuse me, I'm sorry, informal)

Permesso? (pehr-*mehs*-soh) (Excuse me — when walking through a crowded train compartment; also, "May I come in?" when crossing the threshold of someone's house.)

Sì. (see) (Yes.)

No. (noh) (No.)

Basic Question Words in Italian

To communicate in Italian and to travel with ease, there are practical questions in Italian (or any language for that matter) that you'll use daily and have to know:

Parla inglese? (*pahr*-lah een-*gleh*-zeh) (Do you speak English?)

Chi? (kee) (Who?)

Cosa? (*koh*-sah) (What?)

Quando? (*kwahn*-doh) (When?)

Dove? (*doh*-veh) (Where?)

Perché? (pehr-*keh*) (Why?)

Come? (*koh*-meh) (How?)

Quanto? (*kwanh*-toh) (How much?)

Try these helpful phrases:

Dov'è la stazione? (doh-*veh* lah stah-*tsyoh*-neh) (Where is the station?)

Scusi, dov'è il bagno? (*skooh*-zee doh-*veh* eel *bahn*-yoh) (Where is the bathroom?)

Quanto dista il Colosseo? (*kwahn*-toh *dees*-tah eel koh-lohs-*seh*-oh) (How far is the Coloseum?)

Dove si mangia il miglior gelato? (*doh*-veh see *mahn*-jah eel meel-*yohr* geh-*lah*-toh) (Where can you get the best ice cream?)

Come si arriva in Piazza della Repubblica? (*koh*-meh see ahr-*ree*-vah een *pyahts*-sah *dehl*-lah reh-*pooh*-blee-kah) (How do you get to Piazza della Repubblica?)

Days of the Week in Italian

In Italian, the days of the week aren't capitalized. Eyeball this table of the days of the week in Italian (along with pronunciations and abbreviations) to ensure you get your days straight while in Italy.

You might also need to know how to say the following:

Oggi (*ohj*-jee) (today)

Domani (doh-*mah*-nee) (tomorrow)

Dopodomani (*doh*-poh-doh-*mah*-nee) (day after tomorrow)

Ieri (*yeh*-ree) (yesterday)

Getting Help for Emergencies in Italian

If you have an emergency while traveling in Italy, you'll be glad to know these basic Italian phrases. Be prepared for emergencies by committing these Italian phrases to memory:

Aiuto! (ah-*yooh*-toh) (Help!)

Emergenza! (eh-mehr-*jehn*-tsah) (Emergency!)
Chiamate la polizia! (chee-ah-*mah*-teh lah poh-lee-*tsee*-ah) (Call the police!)
Chiamate un'ambulanza! (kee-ah-*mah*-teh ooh-nahm-booh-*lahn*-tsah) (Call an ambulance!)
Ho bisogno di un medico. (oh bee-*zoh*-nyoh dee oohn *meh*-dee-koh) (I need a doctor.)
Dov'è l'ospedale? (doh-*veh* lohs-peh-*dah*-leh) (Where is the hospital?)
Mi sento molto male. (mee *sehn*-toh *mohl*-toh *mah*-leh) (I feel very sick.)

Ordering Food and Drink in Italian

If you visit Italy without trying some of the food, you haven't really visited Italy. (You're also probably rather hungry.) The following phrases can come in handy whether you need a bottle of water or you're ordering a lavish Italian dinner:

Un cappucccino, per favore. (oohn kahp-pooh-*chee*-noh pehr fah-*voh*-reh) (A cappuccino, please.)
Un bicchiere di acqua minerale per favore. (oohn bee-*kyeh*-reh dee *ahk*-wah meen-eh-*rah*-leh perh fah-*voh*-reh). (A glass of mineral water, please.)
Mezzo litro d'acqua. (*mehdz*-zoh *lee*-troh *dahk*-wah) (Half a liter of water.) (Generally, you would take this to go, not standing at the bar)
Mezzo chilo di pesche, per piacere. (*mehdz*-zoh *kee*-loh dee *pehs*-keh perh pyah-*cheh*-reh) (Half a kilo of peaches, please.)
Quanto viene? (*kwahn*-toh *vyeh*-neh) (How much does it come to?)
Un gelato di 2 euro, per favore. (oohn geh-*lah*-toh dee *dooh*-eh *eh*-ooh-roh pehr fah-*voh*-reh) (A 2-Euro size ice cream, please.)
Quali gusti? (*kwah*-lee *goohs*-tee) (What flavors?)
Ci fa il conto, per favore?/Ci porta il conto? (chee fah eel *kohn*-toh pehr fah-*voh*-reh/chee *pohr*-tah eel *kohn*-toh) (Will you bring us the bill please?)

Hotels

In this lesson you'll learn Italian words associated with staying in a hotel.
There's a list of words and translations to study. Now, what could you do to make it more interesting and useful?
Here are some ideas…
– sort the list gramatically, grouping words which are masculine (il) and feminine (la, l')
– sort the list by meaning i.e. the words associated with the hotel bathroom. Why not draw a picture and label it? Attach the result to your fridge to amaze your family and friends!
– group the words by number of syllables and by which syllable is stressed, like this:
2 syllables – 'bag-no, 'do-ccia, 'le-tto'
3 syllables, 1st syllable stressed – 'fri-go-bar
3 syllables, 2nd syllable stressed – al-'ber-go
Once you have your groups of words with the same stress patterns, you could try memorising each group as a chant or a rap, which sounds a little silly at first, but is fun:

beat, beat, 'bag-no, 'do-ccia, 'le-tto, 'vil-la, beat, beat,
l'albergo – hotel
il bagno – bath/bathroom
il parcheggio – parking
la doccia – shower
il frigobar – minibar
la camera singola – single room
la doppia – twin room
la camera matrimoniale – double room
il letto – bed
la coperta – blanket
il cuscino – pillow
la sedia – chair
l'armadio – wardrobe
il portacenere – ashtray
il tavolo – table
la lampada – lamp
il termosifone – radiator
la valigia – suitcase
l'asciugacapelli – hairdrayer
il sapone – soap
la saponetta -bar of soap
la carta igienica – toilet paper
l'asciugamano – towel
il televisore – television
la lavatrice – washing machine
la campagna – countryside
l'aria condizionata – air-conditioning
la villa – villa/residence
il palazzo – building/palace
il quartiere – quarter/district
la colazione – breakfast
la cappella – chapel
la vacanza – holiday
il garage – garage

Environment and Recycling

Recycling, the separation of waste, and caring about the environment are all concepts which have become part of our everyday lives.
Here are some of the key terms relating to these topics:
(nouns)

i rifiuti = l'immondizia [waste]
il riciclaggio [recycling]
la raccolta differenziata [waste separation]
il vetro [glass]
la carta [paper]
la plastica [plastic]
la lattina [can]
il rifiuto umido – l'organico [wet/organic waste]
il cestino [waste basket/bin]
il bidone [larger waste bin]
il cassonetto [large, usually wheeled, waste container]
la discarica [waste dump]
la sporcizia [dirtiness]
la cicca = il mozzicone [cigarette butt]
il suolo [ground]
l'aria [air]
l'ecologia [ecology]
l'inquinamento [pollution]
l'ambiente [environment]
il buco nell'ozono [ozone hole]
la siccità [drought]
la deforestazione [deforestation]
l'effetto serra [greenhouse effect]
(verbs)
rispettare [to respect]
riciclare [to recycle]
inquinare [to pollute]
separare i rifiuti [to sort / to separate wastes]
buttare [to throw out]
gettare [to throw]

Animals

Below is a list of Italian 'animal words', with English translations.
Now, what might you do with it?
Here's a low-tec idea to start with:
1. Get a clean piece of A4 paper
2. Fold it, fold it again, and fold it a third time, so you have eight equal sections
3. Write an 'animal category' title in each section. For example: 'pets', wild animals', 'domestic animals', 'reptiles', 'animals used in food', 'animals used in transport' and so on. The categories can be anything you want. If you can't think of eight, leave a few blank ones – more ideas will come!

4. Go down the list and write the Italian words from the list below in whichever category seems appropriate (some words may go in multiple categories). You choose whether to also add the translations – I wouldn't.

5. Now review your categories. Maybe you only have 'pesce' on its own ('delfino' is a mammal…) In which case, asssuming you care enough, why not go find some more words to accompany it? 'Squalo' is a good one! And any visit to Italy would surely be enhanced were you to acquire an encyclopedic knowledge of terms for fish and seafood…

6. Spend as much time adding words to your categories as pleases you. Online dictionariesa are an obvious resource, but not the only one. For instance, I typed 'wikipedia.it pesce' into my favourite search engine and came up with https://it.wikipedia.org/wiki/Pesce – it's as dense as you'd expect from Wikipedia, but there are some fascinating diagrams with anatomical terms. For beginners, just looking at the pictures is a start – the captions are a rich source of ideas. Or find the word for 'fishing', then look for websites run by or for fishing-enthusiasts…

7. When you're done researching and adding words to your categories, get a pair of scissors and cut your sheet of paper into strips, one for each category.

8. Pick a strip and review the words on it. Do another in a couple of hours, or tomorrow.

9. Put the categories where you have remembered ALL of the words in a separate pile. That way you'll have one pile of categories still to study, and one pile of 'done' categories.

10. When you have remembered all the words in all the categories (good luck), fold up the slips neatly into an envelope, label it 'animali', and make a note to come back to review its contents in a week or so. Bus or train trips are good for this and, wow, you don't even need to be online!

il cane [dog]
il gatto [cat]
il cavallo [horse]
il maiale [pig]
il coniglio [rabbit]
il tacchino [turkey]
il serpente [snake]
il cammello [camel]
l'elefante [elephant]
il pesce [fish]
la pecora [sheep]
il montone [ram]
la mucca [cow]
il toro [bull]
il criceto [hamster]
il delfino [dolphin]
la tartaruga [turtle / tortoise]
il leone [lion]
la farfalla [butterfly]
l'uccello [bird
il ghepardo [cheetah]
la tigre [tiger]
il topo [mouse]
il lupo [wolf]
il cervo [deer]
l'orso [bear]
lo scoiattolo [squirrel]
il cinghiale [wild boar]

l'asino [donkey]
l'anatra [duck]
la balena [whale]
la capra [goat]
il cervo [deer]
la cicogna [stork]
il cinghiale [boar]
il capriolo [roe deer]
il coniglio [rabbit]
il delfino [dolphin]
l'elefante [elephant]
la gallina [hen]
la giraffa [giraffe]
la lumaca [snail]
il lupo [wolf]
l'orso [bear]
il pappagallo [parrot]
la pecora [sheep]
il ragno [spider]
la rana [frog]
il riccio [hedgehog]
la scimmia [ape]
il serpente [snake]
lo squalo [shark]
la tartaruga [turtle]
il topo [mouse]
il verme [worm]
la volpe [fox]
(related words)
le ali [wings]
la gabbia [cage]
il guinzaglio [leash]
la museruola [muzzle]
la piuma [feather]
il pungiglione [stinger]
le zampe [paws]
I bet you could add to this list, with a little immagination and a good online dictionary…
What about, for instance, fur, claws, scales, tentacles, fins, beak, hooves, and so on?
Idiomatic expressions

essere vigliacco come un coniglio [to be as cowardly as a rabbit]
essere la pecore nera della famiglia [to be the black sheep of the family]
avere una memoria da elefante [to have a memory like a elephant]
essere furbo come una volpe [to be as crafty as a fox]
essere lento come una tartaruga [to be as slow as a turtle]
essere intelligente come un delfino [be as smart as a dolphin]

Describing Appearance

In this lesson you will learn some Italian words for describing people's appearance:
aspetto – appearance
gli occhi – eyes
gli occhiali – glasses
castani – brown
blu – blue
azzurri – sky-blue
verdi – green
neri – black
grigi – grey
il naso – nose
piccolo- small
a patata – flat nose
alla francese – snub nose
pulito – neat
grande – big
il sorriso – smile
le orecchie – ears
gli orecchini – earings
i capelli – hair (note that this is plural for Italians, "You have beautiful hairs!")
scuri – dark
chiari – bright
castani – brown
biondi – blond
neri – black
lunghi – long
corti – short
rossi – red
mossi – wavy
lisci – straight
ricci – curly
calvo – bald
rasato – shaved

la barba – beard
i baffi – moustache
alto – tall
basso – short
grasso – fat
magro – thin

STUDY TIP

Write a description of yourself using these verbs and the vocabulary from this lesson:
HO / NON HO
Ho la barba, ho i capelli scuri, non ho gli orecchini…
SONO / NON SONO
Non sono alto, sono magro…
Then try describing someone else you know (don't forget to conjugate the verb to the third person, so ho > ha, sono > è and so on.)
Mia moglie è alta, ha capelli ricci.
il pizzetto [goatee]
le basette [sideboards]
la pelle [skin]
scura [dark]
chiara [pale]
olivastra [olive]
le guance [cheek]
le sopraciglia [eyebrows]
le ciglia [eyelashes]

Bicycle

Below is a short list of Italian words for parts of a bicycle.
la pompa [pump]
la sella [saddle]
il parafango [mudguard]
il campanello [bell]
il manubrio [handlebars]
il freno [brake]
la ruota [wheel]
la gomma [tyre]
i pedali [pedals]
la catena [chain]
The list is far from complete, which is deliberate.
The idea is that you can add to it, with a little research on the internet!

One fun way to do this is to look for Italian websites selling bicycles, and in particular, parts and accessories for bikes.

(If you can't find a retailer, an option which is almost as good is to search for bike rentals in any Italian city you can think of and look at the Italian version of the site...)

Once you find a suitable online shop or other bicycle-related site, clicking through the product categories is a quick and effective way to learn new words, no matter what your level.

I found, for example, 'camera d'aria' (air chamber) – the Italian term for the inflatable rubber tube that goes inside the tyre.

Besides 'data-mining' the new words, read the product descriptions.

These will help you remember the words you're learning IN CONTEXT, and will boost your confidence with reading Italian generally.

And once you're done learning words for parts, why not look at accessories, too? Helmets, baskets, water bottles, I'm sure the list is endless!

Character

Do you know these Italian adjectives for describing a person's character?
Which three best describe YOU? And which ones are you definitely NOT?
aperto [open-minded]
vanitoso [vain]
divertente [funny]
simpatico [nice / likeable]
interessante [interesting]
carino [pretty / cute]
timido [shy]
sensibile [sensitive] – careful, this is a 'false friend'!
intelligente [intelligent]
attraente [attractive / charming]
noioso [boring]
bruttino [ugly]
severo [strict]
loquace [talkative]

Home

Learn Italian words for describing your home and its contents.
la casa – house

il monolocale – studio flat
la mansarda – attic flat
il seminterrato – basement flat
la villa – a large, detached home
l'appartamento – apartment
l'attico – penthouse
il condominio – condominium (USA), block of flats (UK)
il caseggiato – appartment building, block of flats (UK)
il bagno – bathroom
l'asciugacapelli – hairdrier
l'asciugamano – hand towel
il bidet – bidet
la doccia – shower
il lavandino – wash basin
il rubinetto – tap
la vasca – bath
il water – W.C./toilet
la cucina – kitchen
il fornello – cooker
il forno – oven
il frigorifero – fridge
la lavastoviglie – dishwasher
il lavello – sink
la camera – room/bedroom
l'armadio – wardrobe
il comodino – beside table
la coperta – blanket
il letto – bed
la lampada – lamp
la moquette – carpet
lo studio – office
il cestino – trashcan
il computer – computer
la libreria – bookshelves
il portapenne – pencil case
la scrivania – desk
la sedia – chair
la sala/il soggiorno – living room

il divano – couch
la poltrona – armchair
la pianta – plant
il tavolo – table
Here are some more words about the Italian home and its contents!
l'angolo cottura [kitchen area / kitchenette]
il camino [fireplace]
la cucina a gas [gas cooker]
la cucina elettrica [electric cooker]
l'elettrodomestico [household appliance]
il mobile [piece of furniture]
il servizio [bathroom]
la lavastroviglie [dishwasher]

Food

This lesson is about Italian words for food and drink, and also covers definite articles and plurals.
Look at the list of food words at the bottom of this page. You'll see the singular form, the plural form and an English translation.
Do you see how the endings change in the plural? For example:
il pomodor**o** (the tomato), i pomodor**i** (the tomatoes)
And that this is different for masculine and feminine? For example:
la patat**a** (the potato), le patat**e** (the potatoes)
A good starting point is to work out whether a word is masculine or feminine.
Most words ending in -a are feminine, while most words ending in -o are masculine.
Knowing that, you'll need to choose the correct definite article.
In English, the definite article is always 'the'.
But in Italian there are specific definite articles for masculine and feminine nouns.
And confusingly these are different for singular and plural too!
So, 'the' in English could be:
– masculine singular nouns: **il**
(but **l'** before words beginning with a vowel and **lo** before some words beginning with s- or certain other letters and a following consonant)
– masculine plural nouns: **i**
(but **gli** before words beginning with a vowel or before some words beginning with s- or certain other letters and a following consonant)
– feminine singular nouns: **la**
(or **l'** before words beginning with a vowel)
– feminine plural nouns: **le**
It's a lot to take in, isn't it?

Try organising the following list of words into groups according to whether they are masculine and feminine.

Then make lists in each group according to which definite article is used.

This might take you half and hour or so, but will help consolidate the rules for 'the' and plurals, so is an excellent investment of your time!

il peperone, i peperoni – pepper(s) 'FALSE FRIEND' WARNING! ('pepperoni' is not a sausage in Italian)
il pomodoro, i pomodori – tomato(es)
gli spinaci – spinach
la lattuga – lettuce
la rucola – rocket
la zucchina, le zucchine – courgette(s) / zucchini
il cetriolo, i cetrioli – cucumber(s)
la cipolla, le cipolle – onion(s)
l'aglio – garlic
l'oliva, le olive – olive(s)
il broccolo, i broccoli -broccoli
il fagiolo, i fagioli – bean(s)
il mais – sweetcorn
la patata, le patate – potato(es)
la carota, le carote – carrot(s)
il fungo, i funghi – mushroom(s)
la zucca, le zucche – pumpkin(s)
l'insalata, le insalate – salad(s)
la fragola, le fragole – strawberry(ies)
il limone, i limoni – lemon(s)
l'arancia, le arance – orange(s)
la banana, le banane – banana(s)
l'uva – grapes
la mela, le mele – apple(s)
la ciliegia, le ciliegie – cherry(ies)
l'ananas- pineapple
la pesca, le pesche – peach(es)
il lampone, i lamponi – raspberry(ies)
la bacca, le bacche – berry(ies)
la pera, le pere – pear(s)
la prugna, le prugne -plum(s) 'FALSE FRIEND' WARNING! ('prunes' in English are dried plums)
la bibita, le bibite – drink(s)
il caffè, i caffè – coffee(s)
il tè, i tè – tea(s)
il succo, i succhi – juice(s)
la spremuta, le spremute – freshly squeezed fruit juice(s)
lo spumante, gli spumanti – sparkling wine
il vino bianco/rosso, i vini – white/red wine(s)
il ghiaccio – ice

l'acqua – water
il latte – milk
il cornetto, i cornetti – croissant(s)
lo strudel, gli strudel – strudel(s)
il dessert, i dessert – desserts
la carne, le carni – meat(s)
il pesce, i pesci – fish
il tonno, i tonni – tuna
il pollo, i polli – chicken(s)
il prosciutto, i prosciutti – ham(s)
la salsiccia, le salsicce – sausage(s)
il riso – rice
lo spaghetto, gli spaghetti – spaghetti
la tagliatella, le tagliatelle – tagliatelle
la lasagna, le lasagne – lasagne
il toast, i toast – toasted sandwich(es) 'FALSE FRIEND' WARNING! (a snack, not a breakfast food)
il formaggio, i formaggi – cheese(s)
la marmellata, le marmellate – jam(s) 'FALSE FRIEND' WARNING! (marmelade IS jam in Italian!)
il brodo, i brodi – soup(s)
la farina, le farine – flour(s)
l'uovo, le uova – egg(s)
il pane – bread
il gelato, i gelati – icecream(s)
la torta, le torte – cake(s)
la panna, le panne – cream

Cinema

Like movies, films, going to the cinema?

So spend a few minutes learning some words to talk about your passion: director, producer, plot, screenplay, and so on.

Study the vocabulary list below. You'll see the Italian words along with English translations.

Pay particular attention to the articles, as always. 'Il film' or 'la film'? I never remember…

And at the bottom of the page there's an exercise to help you consolidate what you've studied.

lo schermo [screen]
la trama [plot]
l'attore / l'attrice [actor / actress]
la locandina [poster]
il film [film / movie]
il regista [director]
la sceneggiatura [script]
il produttore [producer]
il protagonista [main character]
l'ambientazione [setting]
il cattivo del film [movie's bad guy]

recitare [to act]
filmare [to film]
girare [to shoot a film]
ambientare [to set]

IL GENERE [genre/type]:

Il film ….

d'amore [romantic film]
d'azione [action film]
dell'orrore [horror film]
d'animazione [animated film]
storico [historic film]
drammatico [drama]
d'avventura [adventure film]

la commedia [comedy]

City vs. Countryside

LA CAMPAGNA

l'agricoltura [agriculture]
la coltivazione [cultivation]
la quiete [calmness]

il terreno [ground / soil]
l'orto [vegetable garden]
la fattoria [farm]
il fattore [farmer]
la pianta [plant]
la semina [seeding]
il raccolto [harvest]
la zappa [hoe]
il rastrello [rake]
il trattore [tractor]
l'aratro [plough]
il contadino [farmer / peasant]
il campagnolo [countryman]
l'ortaggio = la verdura [vegetables]

LA CITTÀ

il semaforo [traffic lights]
il pedone [pedestrian]
l'inquinamento [pollution]
il monumento [monument]
la strada [road]
la via [street]
l'abitante [inhabitant]
il turista [tourist]
il sindaco [mayor]
il comune [municipality]
il palazzo = l'edificio [building]
il condominio [block of flats]

Colors

This lesson is about the Italian words for colors, a nice easy vocabulary set to learn.

bianco -white
giallo -yellow
arancione -orange
rosso -red
rosa -pink
viola -violet
azzurro -sky-blue
blu -dark blue
verde – green
marrone – brown
nero -black

Computers

Want to learn some Italian vocabulary on the theme of computers?

Perhaps you work in 'informatica' (what Italians call 'information technology' or I.T.)?

Or maybe you're living in Italy, in which case you'll need to know these terms.

Read through the list below, then try the free exercise.

l'e-mail [e-mail]
il mittente [sender]
il destinatario [addressee]
l'oggetto [subject line]
lo schermo [screen]
la tastiera [keyboard]
il tasto [key / button]
il mouse [computer mouse]
la stampante [printer]
il lettore cd / dvd [CD/DVD player]
l'altoparlante [speaker]
le cuffie [headphones]
il processore [processor]
la scheda di memoria [memory card]
il cavo = il filo [cable]

l'allegato = il file [file]
scaricare [to download]
installare [to install]
salvare [to save]
premere [to press]
inviare = mandare [to send]
alzare il volume [to turn up the volume]
abbassare il volume [to turn down the volume]
ricaricare [to recharge]

Antonyms

In Italian, as in English, opposites of adjectives, nouns or verbs can be formed using different prefixes.

Most of the prefixes used are common to both languages:

anti-
dis-
il-
im-
in-
ir-
s-

I can see one prefix in this list that doesn't seem as if it would be used much in English.

Can you?

Some students and teachers find it helpful to know these 'rules of word formation':

im- is used with words that begin with p-, o- or m-

il- is used with words that begin with l-

ir- is used with words that begin with r-

Here are some examples:

fortunato – sfortunato
approvare – disapprovare

democratico – antidemocratico
discutibile – indiscutibile
rispettoso – irrispettoso
legale – illegale
possibile – impossibile
mortale – immortale

The opposites of some words change completely, rather than being formed with prefixes:

maggioranza – minoranza
educazione – maleducazione
moderno – antico
dolce – amaro

In other cases, rather than using a prefix, or changing the word completely, we just add "non" before the word.

violento – non violento
evidente – non evidente

Below are some further examples of opposites (also known as 'antonyms').

Why not take them, along with the examples above, and organise them in a way that is meaningful to you?

[normal] normale – anormale
[nice] simpatico – antipatico
[democratic] democratico – antidemocratico
[approve] approvare – disapprovare
[approval] consenso – dissenso
[agreement] accordo – disaccordo
[alert] attento – disattento
[pleasure] piacere – dispiacere
[inhibited] inibito – disinibito
[grace] grazia – disgrazia
[attention] attenzione – disattenzione
[interest] interesse – disinteresse
[invest] investire – disinvestire

[lawful] lecito – illecito
[pure] puro – impuro
[mature] maturo – immaturo
[morality] moralità – immoralità
[mortal] mortale – immortale
[effective] efficace – inefficace
[auspicious] fausto – infausto
[balance] equilibrio – inequilibrio
[experience] esperienza – inesperienza
[comprehensible] comprensibile – incomprensibile
[valid] valido – invalido
[safe] sicuro – insicuro
[capable] capace – incapace
[coherent] coerente – incoerente
[dubious] discutibile – indiscutibile
[conceivable] concepibile – inconcepibile
[happiness] felicità – infelicità
[acceptable] accettabile – inaccettabile
[appropriate] adeguato – inadeguato
[national] nazionale – internazionale
[sufficient] sufficiente – insufficiente
[gratitude] gratitudine – ingratitudine
[faithful] fedele – infedele
[corteous] cortese – scortese
[common sense] razionalità – irrazionalità
[regular] regolare – irregolare
[violent] violento – non violento
[post-revolutionary] post-revoluzionario – pre-revoluzionario
[lucky] fortunato – sfortunato
[confidence] fiducia – sfiducia
[to compose] comporre – scomporre
[favour] favore- sfavore
sbagliato – giusto
[benevolent] benevolo – malevolo

[majority] maggioranza – minoranza
[love] amore – odio
[developed] sviluppato – sottosviluppato
[good] buono – cattivo
[dirty] sporco – pulito
[excellent] ottimo – pessimo
[strong] forte – debole
[urban] urbano – interurbano
[daytime] diurno – notturno
[arrival] arrivo – partenza
[included] incluso – escluso
[increase] aumentare – diminuire

Verbs and Nouns for Cooking

This lesson covers Italian words for cooking and meals.

NOUNS
la pentola – pot
il coperchio – lid
la padella – pan
il mestolo – ladle
il cucchiaio di legno – wooden spoon
il colino – colander
il matterello – rolling pin
il cavatappi – corkscrew
il vassoio – tray
la ciotola – bowl
l'insalatiera – salad bowl
le posate – cutlery
il cucchiaio – spoon
il cucchiaino – tea spoon
la forchetta – fork
il coltello – knife

il bicchiere – glass
il piatto – plate

I'm sure your kitchen contains plenty of other useful or essential items that AREN'T listed here (the interns who drew up this list were more familiar with pubs than with kitchens...)

Personally, I couldn't get by without my 'testo', for example. And the 'minipimer' (immersion blender) really comes in handy when I'm preparing a soup...

Why not make a list of your favorite kitchen utensils (checking the Italian words in a good online dictionary) and so personalise the list above?

OK, all ready to cook? You'll need some verbs!

VERBS
cucinare – to cook
pelare – to peel
condire – to dress
aprire – to open
friggere – to fry
tagliare – to cut
scolare – to drain
grattugiare – to grate
bollire/lessare – to boil
affettare – to slice
sbucciare – to peel
versare – to pour
mescolare – to stir/to mix
cuocere nel forno – to bake

Cooking and Baking – Cucinare

Like making cakes and desserts?

On this page you'll find Italian nouns and adjectives for ingredients and kitchen utensils, plus some 'baking' verbs. Yum!

LEARNING TIP: try combining vocabulary-learning and cooking! Start by studying the words on this page. Then research recipes in Italian, choosing something you'd like to make (and eat!) Add new words to your notes. Once you've understood the recipe and assembled the ingredients, switch the oven on and you're ready to go! Repeat (better aloud) the Italian words for the foods and objects you use. Make sentences in your head to describe the actions you are doing, as you do them! The idea is that your brain will associate the new words with the real live objects and actions, so making it easier for you to remember them.

NOUNS
la ciotola [bowl]
il coperchio [cover]
la pentola [pot]
la padella [pan]
il forno [oven]
la temperatura [temperature]

l'ingrediente [ingredient]
il bianco d'uovo/ l'albume [egg white]
il rosso d'uovo/ tuorlo [egg yolk]
la farina [flour]
lo zucchero [sugar]
il lievito [yeast]
l'impasto [dough]

frutti di bosco: [fruits of the forest]:
il mirtillo [blueberry]
la fragola [strawberry]
il lampone [raspberry]
il ribes nero/bianco/rosso [black/ white/ red currants]
la fragolina di bosco [wild strawberry]
la mora [blackberry]

frutta secca: [dried fruit]
la mandorla [almond]
il pistacchio [pistachio]
la noce [walnut]
la nocciola [hazelnut]
l'arachide [peanut]

ADJECTIVES

spesso [thick]

sottile [thin]

liquido [liquid]

denso [dense]

solido [solid]

squisito [delicious]

VERBS

aggiungere [to add]

cuocere in forno [to bake]

impastare [to knead]

mescolare [to mix]

mischiare [to mix]

montare la neve [to whip egg white]

tenere in frigo [to keep in the fridge]

Italian Vocabulary: Describing Food

This lesson is about pairs of words (mostly 'contrari' – opposites) for describing tastes and food:

amaro/ dolce – bitter/sweet

salato/dolce – salty/sweet

gustoso/disgustoso – tasty/disgusting

calorico/dietetico – fattening/ low-calory

cotto/crudo – cooked/raw

condito/scondito – dressed/undressed (for a salad)

leggero/pesante- light/heavy

saporito/insipido – tasty/tasteless

al dente/scotto – firm/overcooked (for pasta)

Which of these words would you use to describe the food in the picture?

Riccardo, a keen student of Italian who lives in the USA, sent me his recipe and photo. Grazie mille, Riccardo!

Many thanks also to Stefi, who checked Riccardo's Italian.

Cous cous con stufato di verdure

Ingredienti:

Melanzana – una (media)
Cuori di carciofo in olio d'oliva – un vasetto da 250 grammi
Olio d'oliva – due cucchiai
Cipolla – 1 cipolla media tritata finemente
Peperone rosso – uno, pulito e tagliato in dadi di 2 cm circa
Zucchine – 2 zucchine piccole, tagliate e tagliate a rondelle di 1 cm di spessore
Aglio – tre spicchi d'aglio
Polpa di pomodoro – 2 lattine
Olive verdi – 12 olive snocciolate e tritate
Basilico – un cucchiaino di basilico secco
Origano – un cucchiaino di origano secco
Peperoncino – mezzo cucchiaino
Cumino – mezzo cucchiaino di cumino macinato
Pepe nero e sale – sale e pepe a piacere
Prezzemolo – 2 cucchiai di prezzemolo fresco tritato

Section (C): Italian Dialogues and Sentences

Italian Conversation 1 – Cambiare i soldi

Learn to understand spoken Italian better with our 'Italian Conversation' series.

Listen to the track below. Try to work out who is speaking and what about. You should listen several times.

If you have time, make notes on details of the conversation. You could even try it as a dictation!

Only when you've understood as much as you can, scroll down the page to find and check the transcript.

Transcript

1. CAMBIARE I SOLDI

Cliente: Buongiorno. Scusi, vorrei cambiare dei soldi.

Impiegato: Che cosa desidera cambiare?

Cliente: Vorrei cambiare 1000 Dollari americani in Euro. Qual è il vostro tasso di cambio?

Impiegato: Il tasso di cambio è di 1,27 Dollari per un Euro. E' molto conveniente.

Cliente: Ci sono commissioni?

Impiegato: La commissione equivale al 2% della somma da cambiare.

Cliente: Va bene, voglio cambiarli.

Impiegato: Attenda un momento, vado alla cassaforte e torno.

Cliente: D'accordo.

Impiegato: Allora 1000 dollari americani sono 787 euro. Ecco a lei.

Cliente: Grazie mille. Avete anche gli yen giapponesi?

Impiegato: Al momento no, ma possiamo ordinarli. Arriveranno qui entro martedì, se non ha fretta. Il loro tasso di cambio è di 109 Yen per un dollaro americano.

Cliente: La ringrazio. Vorrei acquistare degli Yen perché la prossima settimana dovrò andare a Tokyo per un viaggio di lavoro. Verrò martedì allora.

Impiegato: La ringrazio molto!

Cliente: Arrivederci

Italian Conversation 2 – Riparare la macchina

Learn to understand spoken Italian better with our 'Italian Conversation' series.

Listen to the track below. Try to work out who is speaking and what about. You should listen several times.

If you have time, make notes on details of the conversation. You could even try it as a dictation!

Only when you've understood as much as you can, scroll down the page to check the transcript.

Transcript

2. RIPARARE LA MACCHINA

Maria: Pronto scusi, parlo con il meccanico?

Meccanico: Sì pronto, mi dica.

Maria: Salve, mi chiamo Maria, chiamo perché la mia macchina si è fermata lungo la tangenziale a Milano. Non so qual è il problema, potrebbe mandare un carro attrezzi?

Meccanico: Mi dica dove si trova e le manderò un carro attrezzi in un'ora.

Maria: Sono al chilometro 20 della tangenziale

Meccanico: A tra poco
—–

Meccanico: Allora ho controllato la sua macchina, purtroppo ha il radiatore rotto. Posso Ripararla ma ci vorrà qualche giorno.

Maria: Davvero? Perché a me servirebbe subito la macchina.

Meccanico: Non si preoccupi, le posso dare l'auto di cortesia.

Maria: La ringrazio. Quando posso tornare a riprendere la macchina?

Meccanico: Torni pure martedì prossimo dopo le cinque.

Maria: D'accordo.

Italian Conversation 3 – Noleggio macchine bici

Learn to understand spoken Italian better with our 'Italian Conversation' series.

Listen to the track below. Try to work out who is speaking and what about. You should listen several times.

If you have time, make notes on details of the conversation. You could even try it as a dictation!

Only when you've understood as much as you can, scroll down the page to check the transcript.

Transcript

3. NOLEGGIO MACCHINE/BICI

Cliente: Buongiorno, vorrei noleggiare un'auto per tre giorni.

Impiegato: Buongiorno, che tipo di auto desidera?

Cliente: Vorrei un'utilitaria che non consumi troppo.

Impiegato: Allora per lei abbiamo due modelli tra cui scegliere. Le mostro il catalogo.

Cliente: Grazie, penso che prenderò questa Ford. Quant'è il costo del noleggio?

Impiegato: Sono 70 euro al giorno più il costo della benzina.

Cliente: Grazie allora la prendo.

Impiegato: Mi dia la sua patente per favore. Faccio una fotocopia e gliela riporto.

Cliente: Ecco a lei.

Impiegato: Grazie, allora può passare a ritirare la macchina in garage. Buona giornata.

Cliente: Arrivederci.

—

Impiegato: Buongiorno

Cliente: Buongiorno, vorrei noleggiare una bici. Quanto costa?

Impiegato: Costa 15 € al giorno. Desidera anche noleggiare il casco?

Cliente: Sì grazie.

Impiegato: Venga con me a scegliere la bici che preferisce.

Cliente: La ringrazio.

Italian Conversation 4 – Al Bar

Learn to understand spoken Italian better with our 'Italian Conversation' series.

Listen to the track below. Try to work out who is speaking and what about. You should listen several times.

If you have time, make notes on details of the conversation. You could even try it as a dictation!

Only when you've understood as much as you can, scroll down the page to check the transcript.

Transcript

4. AL BAR

Barista: Buongiorno!

Cliente: Buongiorno.

Barista: Cosa desidera?

Cliente: Vorrei un cappuccino e un cornetto.

Barista: Che tipo di cornetto?

Cliente: Con la crema.

Barista: Va bene. Sono due euro. Grazie mille.

—-

Barista: Buonasera.

Cliente: Salve, io e i miei amici vorremmo fare un aperitivo.

Barista: Prego, accomodatevi ai tavoli.

Cliente: Cosa ci consiglia?

Barista: Consiglio l'aperitivo della casa. E' composto da un bicchiere di prosecco della zona, delle olive, delle noccioline, delle patatine fritte e delle pizzette.

Cliente: Perfetto, allora ci porti cinque aperitivi della casa. E' permesso fumare?

Barista: Sì nei tavoli all'esterno del locale è permesso fumare.

Italian Conversation 5 – Pizza d'asporto

Learn to understand spoken Italian better with our 'Italian Conversation' series.

Listen to the track below. Try to work out who is speaking and what about. You should listen several times.

If you have time, make notes on details of the conversation. You could even try it as a dictation!

Only when you've understood as much as you can, scroll down the page to check the transcript.

Transcript

5. PIZZA D'ASPORTO

Cliente: Pronto, parlo con la pizzeria Da Vincenzo?

Cameriere: Sì, salve mi dica.

Cliente: Vorrei ordinare delle pizze per stasera.

Cameriere: Che tipo di pizze vuole?

Cliente: Vorrei una pizza Napoli, una margherita e una capricciosa. Vorrei anche una porzione di patatine fritte.

Cameriere: D'accordo, per che ora?

Cliente: Per le otto e mezza. Effettuate servizio a domicilio o devo passare a prenderle?

Cameriere: No, possiamo consegnarle noi. Mi dia il suo nome e indirizzo.

Cliente: Sono Claudio Rossi e abito in via Amerigo Vespucci 134.

Cameriere: Mi può lasciare il suo numero di telefono?

Cliente: Certo. Il mio numero è 334-4545670.

Cameriere: La ringrazio, a più tardi.

Cliente: Grazie e arrivederci.

—

Cliente: Pronto, chiamo per ordinare delle pizze.

Cameriere: Si, mi dica che pizze vuole.

Cliente: Vorrei una pizza margherita e una pizza con i funghi.

Cameriere: A che ora vuole passare a ritirarle?

Cliente: Passerò per le otto.

Cameriere: La ringrazio, a dopo.

Italian Conversation 6 – Prenotare un ristorante

Learn to understand spoken Italian better with our 'Italian Conversation' series.

Listen to the track below. Try to work out who is speaking and what about. You should listen several times.

If you have time, make notes on details of the conversation. You could even try it as a dictation!

Only when you've understood as much as you can, scroll down the page to check the transcript.

Transcript

6. PRENOTARE UN RISTORANTE

Cliente: Pronto parlo con il ristorante Il Veliero?

Cameriere: Si, mi dica.

Cliente: Vorrei prenotare un tavolo per sei persone stasera verso le otto e mezza.

Cameriere: Va bene, mi dia il suo nome.

Cliente: Il mio nome è Gianluca Tozzi. Mi scusi, qual è il piatto del giorno?

Cameriere: Il piatto del giorno è zuppa di pesce fresco.

Cliente: La ringrazio a più tardi.

—

Cliente: Salve, sono venuta per prenotare il vostro ristorante per la mia festa di compleanno. Siamo circa 50 persone.

Cameriere: D'accordo, mi dica per quale giorno.

Cliente: Per il 27 settembre.

Cameriere: Aspetti che controllo. Sì il 27 settembre è libero.

Cliente: Avete dei menù fissi?

Cameriere: Sì, in genere per i compleanni abbiamo il menù fisso da 20 € compresa la torta.

Cliente: Va benissimo, allora prenoto per il 27.

Cameriere: Certo, mi dica il suo nome.

Cliente: Greta Bianchi. Le devo lasciare un acconto?

Cameriere: No, non si preoccupi.

Cliente: Arrivederci.

Italian Conversation 7 – Street food

Learn to understand spoken Italian better with our 'Italian Conversation' series.

Listen to the track below. Try to work out who is speaking and what about. You should listen several times.

If you have time, make notes on details of the conversation. You could even try it as a dictation!

Only when you've understood as much as you can, scroll down the page to check the transcript.

Transcript

7. STREET FOOD (Due tipiche cose che si vendono a Roma...)

Cliente: Buongiorno, quanto viene uno zucchero filato?

Venditore: Due euro lo zucchero bianco e due euro e cinquanta quello rosa o azzurro.

Cliente: Mia figlia vorrebbe quello rosa, grazie.

Venditore: Aspetti due minuti che lo preparo. Ecco, sono due euro e cinquanta centesimi.

Cliente: Mi scusi ma quelle noccioline sono calde?

Venditore: Sì, sono calde.

Cliente: Allora mi dia anche un po' di quelle. Quant'è in tutto?

Venditore: In totale sono 4 euro.

Cliente: Ecco a lei.

Venditore: Grazie. Arrivederla.

—

Cliente: Buongiorno, mi da un trancio di pizza margherita?

Venditore: Come la vuole? Con l'angolo o senza?

Cliente: Meglio senza.

Venditore: D'accordo, un attimo che gliela scaldo.

Cliente: OK.

Venditore: A lei, sono un euro e cinquanta centesimi, grazie.

Italian Conversation 8 – Al pub

Learn to understand spoken Italian better with our 'Italian Conversation' series.

Listen to the track below. Try to work out who is speaking and what about. You should listen several times.

If you have time, make notes on details of the conversation. You could even try it as a dictation!

Only when you've understood as much as you can, scroll down the page to check the transcript.

Transcript

8. AL PUB

Cliente 1: In questo nuovo pub le birre sono molto buone. Ci sono stato ieri con un'amica.

Cliente 2: Davvero? Che birra mi consigli?

Cliente 1: Consiglio di prendere una birra artigianale della casa.

Cliente 2: Seguirò il tuo consiglio. Tu che prendi?

Cliente 1: Io prendo una birra scura. Cameriere! Per favore ci porta una birra della casa e una birra scura? Grazie.

—

Cliente: Buonasera.

Cameriere: Buonasera, cosa desideri ordinare?

Cliente: Che birre avete questa settimana?

Cameriere: Abbiamo un'ottima birra belga, non troppo forte. Altrimenti una birra tedesca più forte.

Cliente: Va bene quella belga.

Cameriere: E da mangiare?

Cliente: Una porzione di patatine fritte ed un hamburger ben cotto.

Cameriere: Basta così?

Cliente: Sì grazie.

Cameriere: Arrivo subito con le ordinazioni.

Italian Conversation 9. La ricerca della scuola di lingua italiana

Learn to understand spoken Italian better with our 'Italian Conversation' series.

Listen to the track below. Try to work out who is speaking and what about. You should listen several times.

If you have time, make notes on details of the conversation. You could even try it as a dictation!

Only when you've understood as much as you can, scroll down the page to check the transcript.

Transcript

9. RICERCA DELLA SCUOLA DI LINGUA ITALIANA

Cliente: Salve parlo con la scuola di lingua Madrelingua?

Impiegato: Sì salve, come posso aiutarla?

Cliente: Sto cercando una scuola di lingua a Bologna. Sono inglese e verrò a Bologna questa estate per studiare l'italiano. Vorrei stare dalla metà di giugno alla fine di luglio. Avete dei corsi per quel periodo?

Impiegato: Un attimo che controllo... no, mi spiace, non ci saranno corsi nuovi per quel periodo perché le iscrizioni sono poche.

Cliente: Ho capito. Mi sa dire quale scuola posso chiamare?

Impiegato: Può chiamare la nostra sede di via San Giorgio, sicuramente lì ci saranno dei corsi estivi.

Cliente: Può darmi il numero di telefono?

Impiegato: Sì, il numero è 051/267822.

Cliente: Grazie, a presto.
...
Cliente: Pronto è la scuola Madrelingua di via San Giorgio?

Impiegato: Sì mi dica.

Cliente: Vorrei sapere se ci saranno corsi estivi di italiano.

Impiegato: Sì ci sono corsi nei mesi di luglio, agosto e settembre. Il costo di un corso di un mese è 400 euro. Si può iscrivere al corso sul nostro sito internet.

Cliente: La ringrazio molto!

Impiegato: Si figuri, arrivederci.

Italian Conversation 10. Prenotazione di una scuola di italiano

Learn to understand spoken Italian better with our 'Italian Conversation' series.

Listen to the track below. Try to work out who is speaking and what about. You should listen several times.

If you have time, make notes on details of the conversation. You could even try it as a dictation!

Only when you've understood as much as you can, scroll down the page to check the transcript.

Transcript

10. PRENOTAZIONE DI UNA SCUOLA D'ITALIANO

Cliente: Salve, sono venuto ad iscrivermi ad un corso di lingua italiana.

Impiegato: Che tipo di corso cerca?

Cliente: Vorrei fare un corso avanzato di conversazione.

Impiegato: Bene, il corso è il martedì e il giovedì dalle 9 alle 13.

Cliente: Come mi posso iscrivere?

Impiegato: Deve compilare questo modulo di iscrizione. Deve scrivere nome, cognome, numero di telefono e il tipo di corso che vuole fare. Poi alla fine deve firmarlo.

Cliente: Fatto, e poi?

Impiegato: Ora deve solo effettuare il pagamento. Deve fare un bonifico sul conto corrente della scuola e portarci la ricevuta. Il numero del conto è 130459039949999 e l'intestatario è Scuola di Lingua Italiana. Può fare il bonifico in qualsiasi banca o su internet.

Cliente: Ho capito, e poi?

Impiegato: Poi può venire a seguire i nostri corsi.

Cliente: OK, grazie mille!

Impiegato: Di niente, si figuri!

Italian Conversation 11, Scuola d'italiano: sistemazione

Learn to understand spoken Italian better with our 'Italian Conversation' series.

Listen to the track below. Try to work out who is speaking and what about. You should listen several times.

If you have time, make notes on details of the conversation. You could even try it as a dictation!

Only when you've understood as much as you can, scroll down the page to check the transcript.

Transcript

11. Scuola d'italiano: sistemazione

Cliente: Salve, parlo con la scuola di italiano?

Impiegata: Sì, salve, sono Giulia, come posso aiutarla?

Cliente: Allora, io mi sono iscritta al vostro corso di italiano estivo. Volevo sapere se potete aiutarmi a trovare un alloggio per quei mesi.

Impiegata: Sì, non si preoccupi, abbiamo anche un servizio di ricerca di stanze. Preferisce stare in una stanza singola o in una doppia?

Cliente: Preferisco una stanza singola. Non vorrei dividere la camera con qualcuno che non conosco.

Impiegata: Ho capito. Le stanze singole in genere sono più care. Può scegliere se stare in una stanza singola all'interno dello studentato della scuola oppure stare presso una famiglia italiana.
Il prezzo è di circa 350 euro al mese per lo studentato e di 400 euro per stare in famiglia, poiché sono inclusi anche i pasti. Nello studentato invece può usare la cucina e fare la spesa da solo.

Cliente: Ho capito. Allora preferisco stare in famiglia per esercitare la lingua.

Impiegata: Allora le invio per email la domanda per chiedere l'alloggio in famiglia. Nell'email troverà anche tutte le informazioni del caso. Va bene?

Cliente: D'accordo, la ringrazio. Arrivederci.

Impiegata: Si figuri, a presto.

Italian Conversation 12, Scuola d'italiano: home stay

Learn to understand spoken Italian better with our 'Italian Conversation' series.

Listen to the track below. Try to work out who is speaking and what about. You should listen several times.

If you have time, make notes on details of the conversation. You could even try it as a dictation!

Only when you've understood as much as you can, scroll down the page to check the transcript.

Transcript

12. Scuola d'italiano: home stay

Lukas: Salve, sono appena arrivato dalla Germania. Mi chiamo Lukas e sono uno studente dei corsi estivi. Ho scelto di soggiornare in famiglia.

Impiegata: Salve, ben arrivato, controllo subito. Allora, sì Lukas, la tua famiglia ospitante sono i Rossi. Vivono poco lontano dal centro. Li chiamo subito, verranno a prenderti loro qui per accompagnarti a casa.

—

Signora Rossi: Ciao Lukas, io sono Lucia e questo è mio marito Marco. Ti mostro la tua stanza. Come vedi è abbastanza grande e c'è anche un armadio. Il bagno è in fondo a destra.

Lukas: Grazie mille.

Signora Rossi: Allora, noi ceniamo ogni sera alle otto e mezza. Per favore avverti se non vieni a cena. Per quanto riguarda il pranzo?

Lukas: Grazie, ma pranzerò alla mensa della scuola perché ho lezione anche il pomeriggio.

Signora Rossi: Allora, queste sono le chiavi di casa. Se hai bisogno di qualcosa, per favore facci sapere, ok?

Lukas: Un'ultima domanda: come posso arrivare alla scuola con l'autobus?

Signora Rossi: Allora, percorri la via fino in fondo e poi gira a destra. Dopo 100 metri troverai la metropolitana.

Lukas: Grazie.

Italian Conversation 13. Scuola d'italiano: primo giorno in classe

Learn to understand spoken Italian better with our 'Italian Conversation' series.

Listen to the track below. Try to work out who is speaking and what about. You should listen several times.

If you have time, make notes on details of the conversation. You could even try it as a dictation!

Only when you've understood as much as you can, scroll down the page to check the transcript.

Transcript

13. Scuola d'italiano: primo giorno in classe

Insegnante: Buongiorno a tutti, mi chiamo Angela e sono la vostra insegnante di italiano. Nei tre mesi di corso di conversazione che ci aspettano, parleremo di molti argomenti. Siccome in classe ci sono studenti da tutte le parti del mondo, a lezione parleremo solo in lingua italiana. Ci sono domande?

Studente: Scusi professoressa, ci saranno anche lezioni di grammatica?

Insegnante: Allora, questo è un corso di conversazione. Però per parlare bene una lingua bisogna conoscere anche la grammatica, quindi ogni tanto faremo lezione di grammatica.

Studente: Le lezioni si fanno sempre in classe?

Insegnante: Di solito le lezioni si fanno in quest'aula. Però a metà corso mi piacerebbe fare una lezione al museo. In quell'occasione potrete ascoltare la guida e fare domande.

Studente: Scusi, ma ci sarà un esame alla fine del corso?

Insegnante: Alla fine del corso potrete decidere se fare l'esame. Io ve lo consiglio... Allora, se non ci sono altre domande, cominciamo! Direi di iniziare con le presentazioni. Ognuno di voi deve alzarsi in piedi e presentarsi ai compagni...

Italian Conversation 14. Scuola d'italiano: chiedere aiuto

Learn to understand spoken Italian better with our 'Italian Conversation' series.

Listen to the track below. Try to work out who is speaking and what about. You should listen several times.

If you have time, make notes on details of the conversation. You could even try it as a dictation!

Only when you've understood as much as you can, scroll down the page to check the transcript.

Transcript

14. Scuola d'italiano: chiedere aiuto

Studentessa: Salve, sono una studentessa della vostra scuola, ho un problema, posso chiedere a lei?

Impiegata: Sì dimmi, sono la responsabile degli studenti.

Studentessa: Allora, io sono iscritta al corso estivo di italiano, ma ho l'impressione che il livello sia troppo basso per me, vorrei cambiare.

Impiegata: Vorresti passare a un corso più difficile?

Studentessa: Sì, grazie.

Impiegata: Allora dobbiamo parlarne con l'insegnante del corso. Di sicuro dovrai fare un piccolo esame di accesso per vedere se il livello più alto è adatto, d'accordo?

Studentessa: Va bene, quando posso fare questo esame?

Impiegata: Domani alle tre, in aula 2 ci sarà l'insegnante. Puoi chiedere a lei. Si chiama Gilda Rubino.

Studentessa: Grazie.

Studentessa: Scusi, ho un problema con gli orari però... Ho iniziato un piccolo lavoro part-time e non posso più frequentare i corsi della mattina. Ci sono corsi serali?

Impiegata: Certo. Può passare ai corsi serali, dalle 18 alle 21. Devo controllare se c'è posto. Un attimo... bene, non ci sono problemi. Compili questa domanda e dalla settimana prossima potrà seguire le lezioni serali.

Studentessa: Grazie.

Italian Conversation 15. Internet Cafè

Learn to understand spoken Italian better with our 'Italian Conversation' series.

Listen to the track below. Try to work out who is speaking and what about. You should listen several times.

If you have time, make notes on details of the conversation. You could even try it as a dictation!

Only when you've understood as much as you can, scroll down the page to check the transcript.

Transcript

15. Internet Cafè

Commessa: Buongiorno, mi dica.

Cliente: Buongiorno, volevo sapere se era possibile usare i computer

Commessa: Certo, al momento c'è una postazione vuota. Ha la tessera?

Cliente: No, è la prima volta che vengo.

Commessa: Allora, deve compilare questo modulo con i suoi dati e mettere una firma alla fine.

Cliente: OK.

Commessa: Bene, questa è la sua tessera. Quando arriva al computer deve inserire la tessera per andare su internet. Appena inserisce la tessera deve creare il suo account e inserire una password.

Cliente: Grazie. E quanto costa usare internet?

Commessa: Sono 25 centesimi ogni 15 minuti. In pratica costa 1 euro l'ora.

Cliente: Posso stampare dei documenti?

Commessa: Sì, è possibile stampare. Il costo è di venti centesimi per una stampa in bianco e nero e di cinquanta centesimi per una a colori. Si ricordi, se scarica qualche documento, di cancellarlo prima di andarsene.

Cliente: Ho capito, grazie.

Commessa: Può accomodarsi alla postazione due, in fondo al corridoio sulla sinistra. Per qualsiasi problema sono a sua disposizione.

Cliente: Grazie mille.

Italian Conversation 16. Ufficio postale (mandare/ricevere un pacco)

Learn to understand spoken Italian better with our 'Italian Conversation' series.

Listen to the track below. Try to work out who is speaking and what about. You should listen several times.

If you have time, make notes on details of the conversation. You could even try it as a dictation!

Only when you've understood as much as you can, scroll down the page to check the transcript.

Transcript

16. Ufficio postale (mandare/ricevere un pacco)

Cliente: Buongiorno, ho trovato questo avviso nella mia cassetta delle lettere. Dice che c'è un pacco per me da ritirare.

Impiegata: Buongiorno, mi faccia vedere l'avviso... ok, è lei Lucia Rossi?

Cliente: Sì sono io.

Impiegata: Può darmi un documento d'identità?

Cliente: Eccolo.

Impiegata: Va bene grazie, attenda qui... ecco questo è il suo pacco. Per favore firmi qui per la ricevuta.

Cliente: Fatto, grazie.

Impiegata: Grazie a lei.

—-

Cliente: Buongiorno, dovrei spedire questo pacco.

Impiegata: Buongiorno, vuole spedirlo tramite posta prioritaria o posta ordinaria?

Cliente: Che differenza c'è?

Impiegata: Con la posta prioritaria il pacco arriva in tre giorni, con quella ordinaria in dieci giorni.

Cliente: Ah, ho capito, allora scelgo la posta prioritaria.

Impiegata: Va bene, allora compili questi moduli con l'indirizzo. Intanto mi dia il pacco. Il peso è di tre chili. Spedirlo costa 18 euro e 50.

Cliente: Ecco a lei.

Impiegata: Grazie, ecco il resto, arrivederci.

Cliente: Arrivederci.

Italian Conversation 17. Problemi, Dottore

Learn to understand spoken Italian better with our 'Italian Conversation' series.

Listen to the track below. Try to work out who is speaking and what about. You should listen several times.

If you have time, make notes on details of the conversation. You could even try it as a dictation!

Only when you've understood as much as you can, scroll down the page to check the transcript.

Transcript

17.PROBLEMI: DOTTORE

Paziente: Buongiorno

Dottoressa: Salve, qual è il problema?

Paziente: Non mi sento bene. Ho un gran mal di gola, mal di testa e raffreddore. Questa notte ho dormito malissimo, avevo sempre freddo.

Dottoressa: Ha anche dolore alle ossa?

Paziente: Sì, mi sento dolorante.

Dottoressa: Aspetti che la visito… ha la gola tutta arrossata e ha anche un po' di febbre. Lei ha preso l'influenza stagionale e le tonsille sono infiammate. Le prescrivo dei medicinali da prendere mattina e sera. Poi deve anche usare questo spray per la gola. Se la febbre sale prenda del paracetamolo. Per il resto, stia a letto e si riposi. Guarirà in pochi giorni.

Paziente: Grazie arrivederci.

—

Paziente: Buongiorno dottoressa.

Dottoressa: Salve mi dica.

Paziente: Ieri sono caduto e mi sono fatto male alla caviglia. Adesso è tutta gonfia e mi fa malissimo. Ci ho messo il ghiaccio ma non è passato.

Dottoressa: Mi faccia vedere… mmmh è molto gonfia, potrebbe essere rotta. Deve andare al pronto soccorso per fare una lastra e vedere cosa è successo.

Paziente: Va bene, la ringrazio.

Dottoressa: Arrivederci e mi faccia sapere!

Italian Conversation 18. Problemi, Dentista

Learn to understand spoken Italian better with our 'Italian Conversation' series.

Listen to the track below. Try to work out who is speaking and what about. You should listen several times.

If you have time, make notes on details of the conversation. You could even try it as a dictation!

Only when you've understood as much as you can, scroll down the page to check the transcript.

Transcript

18. Problemi, Dentista

Paziente: Buongiorno Dottore.

Dentista: Buongiorno, mi dica.

Paziente: Mi fa malissimo un dente, non riesco nemmeno a mangiare.

Dentista: Si sieda sulla sedia e apra la bocca, così controllo. Allora, ecco, lei ha un ascesso. E' una brutta infezione, dovrò operarla.

Paziente: Quando posso venire?

Dentista: Può venire domani mattina presto.

Paziente: Grazie.

—

Paziente: Buongiorno dottore.

Dentista: Buongiorno signora Carli. E' qui per il controllo? Si sieda e apra la bocca. Allora, mi sembra che vada quasi tutto bene, ma ha una piccola carie su un dente, sarebbe bene curarla subito.

Paziente: Davvero? E quando posso venire?

Dentista: Prenda appuntamento con la segretaria per quando preferisce, non c'è fretta. Inoltre ci vorrà poco tempo.

Paziente: Grazie dottore, arrivederci.

Dentista: Grazie a lei.

Italian Conversation 19. Raccontare una crimine

Learn to understand spoken Italian better with our 'Italian Conversation' series.

Listen to the track below. Try to work out who is speaking and what about. You should listen several times.

If you have time, make notes on details of the conversation. You could even try it as a dictation!

Only when you've understood as much as you can, scroll down the page to check the transcript.

Transcript

19. Problemi – Raccontare una crimine

Polizia: Pronto, centrale di polizia di Roma Eur.

Lucia: Pronto, sono Lucia Rossi, chiamo dalla stazione Termini. Volevo dirle che due uomini hanno derubato una donna e sono scappati via! La donna è caduta a terra e si è fatta male, adesso è andata in ospedale.

Polizia: Lei ha visto l'accaduto?

Lucia: Sì, è successo davanti ai miei occhi.

Polizia: Può descriverci come erano i ladri?

Lucia: I ladri erano due uomini, un ragazzo di circa venti anni e un uomo sui quaranta. Indossavano entrambi dei jeans scuri. Il giovane aveva un cappotto bianco e indossava un cappello di lana nero. L'altro aveva la barba e i capelli lunghi e indossava un cappotto di pelle marrone. Sono scappati di corsa verso via Marsala.

Polizia: Quanto tempo fa è successo?

Lucia: Circa dieci minuti fa. Un passante ha provato ad inseguirli per fermarli.

Polizia: Abbiamo appena avvisato i nostri colleghi di Via Marsala, che andranno sul posto.

Lucia: Ho capito, grazie.

Polizia: Grazie a lei.

Italian Conversation 20. Problemi, Chiedere aiuto

Learn to understand spoken Italian better with our 'Italian Conversation' series.

Listen to the track below. Try to work out who is speaking and what about. You should listen several times.

If you have time, make notes on details of the conversation. You could even try it as a dictation!

Only when you've understood as much as you can, scroll down the page to check the transcript.

Transcript

20. Problemi, Chiedere aiuto

Lukas: Buongiorno signora, mi scusi, può aiutarmi?

Signora: Sì mi dica.

Lukas: Salve mi chiamo Lukas, sono uno studente tedesco in vacanza in Italia. Mi sono perso. Devo raggiungere la piazza dove si trovano i miei amici, ma ho sbagliato strada.

Signora: In che piazza deve andare?

Lukas: Non ricordo bene. Vorrei chiamarli, ma il telefono si è scaricato e si è spento.

Signora: Puoi usare il mio telefono.

Lukas: Davvero? Grazie, lei è molto gentile.

Signora: Si figuri.

—

Carla: Buongiorno. Scusi ma la mia amica non si sente bene! Qualcuno può chiamare un medico?

Barista: Che cos'ha?

Carla: E' svenuta, adesso si è un po' ripresa, ma è ancora debole.

Barista: Portale questo bicchiere d'acqua e poi accompagnala qui. Io chiamo l'ambulanza.

Carla: Grazie, vado subito.

Italian Conversation 21. Problemi, Perdere il bagaglio

Learn to understand spoken Italian better with our 'Italian Conversation' series.

Listen to the track below. Try to work out who is speaking and what about. You should listen several times.

If you have time, make notes on details of the conversation. You could even try it as a dictation!

Only when you've understood as much as you can, scroll down the page to check the transcript.

Transcript

21. Problemi, Perdere il bagaglio

Impiegata: Buongiorno, qui è l'ufficio per i bagagli smarriti.

Mark: Buongiorno, io sono atterrato questa mattina alle nove e venti con il volo AX345 da Vancouver e adesso sono le tre del pomeriggio e ancora non ho ricevuto il mio bagaglio.

Impiegata: Strano, i bagagli del volo AX345 sono arrivati alle 10 e 20. Mi dice il suo nome?

Mark: Mi chiamo Scott Mark.

Impiegata: Vado a controllare in magazzino se è arrivato in un altro terminal e nessuno l'ha preso. Attenda... nel magazzino non c'è un bagaglio con il suo nome. Il suo bagaglio deve essere stato smarrito. Allora, bisogna fare una denuncia di smarrimento. Deve compilare questo modulo.

Mark: Ho capito, ma è possibile trovarlo?

Impiegato: Non si preoccupi, facciamo subito domanda agli altri aeroporti per sapere se magari è arrivato per sbaglio in un'altra città. Comunque, lei ha un'assicurazione sul bagaglio?

Mark: Sì, ho fatto un'assicurazione per i casi di furto e smarrimento.

Impiegata: Benissimo, allora deve contattare la sua assicurazione. Con il modulo di denuncia ha diritto ad un rimborso. Comunque ci lasci i suoi recapiti, se lo troviamo la chiamiamo subito.

Mark: Grazie.

Italian Conversation 22. Problemi, Venire arrestato

Learn to understand spoken Italian better with our 'Italian Conversation' series.

Listen to the track below. Try to work out who is speaking and what about. You should listen several times.

If you have time, make notes on details of the conversation. You could even try it as a dictation!

Only when you've understood as much as you can, scroll down the page to check the transcript.

Transcript

22. Problemi, Venire arrestato

Agente: Buongiorno, sicurezza dell'aeroporto di Fiumicino, mi fa vedere il suo documento?

Luca: Salve, ecco il mio passaporto.

Agente: Facciamo un controllo… mi dispiace signore, ma questo non è il suo passaporto, questo passaporto risulta rubato. Ci deve seguire in centrale.

Luca: Ma come? Che dite? Io non ho rubato niente! E' il mio passaporto! Ci deve essere uno sbaglio!

Agente: Ci segua.

…

Agente: Allora, perché ci ha mostrato un documento rubato, signor Foschi?

Luca: Ma io non sono il signor Foschi! Io mi chiamo Luca Pratesi. Lo può vedere sui miei documenti.

Agente: Mi dispiace, ma quello che ci ha dato è un passaporto senza foto e c'è scritto che si chiama Matteo Foschi.

Luca: Non è il mio passaporto!

Agente: Allora di chi è? Perché ce l'ha mostrato?

Luca: Io ho solo preso il passaporto dalla mia borsa.

Agente: E' questa la sua borsa?

Luca: Sì... anzi no, la mia borsa è simile a quella, ma non è quella, devo averla scambiata con quella del passeggero vicino a me in aereo. Erano tutte e due borse nere, credetemi!

Agente: Allora deve aspettare qui finché non facciamo tutti i controlli, mi spiace.

Italian Conversation 23. Problemi, Avere un crollo

Learn to understand spoken Italian better with our 'Italian Conversation' series.

Listen to the track below. Try to work out who is speaking and what about. You should listen several times.

If you have time, make notes on details of the conversation. You could even try it as a dictation!

Only when you've understood as much as you can, scroll down the page to check the transcript.

Transcript

23. Problemi, Avere un crollo

Carla: Pronto Luisa, sono Carla.

Luisa: Ciao Carla come stai?

Carla: Non sto per niente bene, puoi venire prima che puoi qui da me?

Luisa: Carla, mi devo preoccupare?

Carla: Sto avendo un esaurimento nervoso, ho bisogno di qualcuno con cui parlare.

Luisa: Arrivo.

—

Luisa: Carla come stai?

Carla: Ciao Luisa, sto malissimo. A lavoro sono molto stressata, il mio capo mi tratta male ed è sempre nervoso. Ho paura che voglia licenziarmi, quindi per la prossima riunione devo portare un bel progetto per dimostrare che sono un bravo architetto, sono proprio sotto pressione!

Luisa: Ho capito, è una situazione difficile... come ti senti?

Carla: Molto male. Ho una grande ansia, ho mal di testa e mi tremano le mani.

Luisa: Ho capito Carla, è proprio un crollo nervoso. Allora adesso devi metterti a letto e cercare di riposare. Io ti preparo una camomilla. Dopo che hai dormito un po', usciamo a divertirci, così ti distrai, va bene?

Carla: Va bene, ci provo. Grazie Luisa, sei una vera amica.

Luisa: Non ti preoccupare. In questi casi un po' di risposo è la medicina più efficace. Vai pure a riposarti.

Italian Conversation 24. Problemi, Restare coinvolto in un incidente

Learn to understand spoken Italian better with our 'Italian Conversation' series.

Listen to the track below. Try to work out who is speaking and what about. You should listen several times.

If you have time, make notes on details of the conversation. You could even try it as a dictation!

Only when you've understood as much as you can, scroll down the page to check the transcript.

Transcript

24. Problemi, Restare coinvolto in un incidente

Fabio: Pronto parlo con I vigili urbani?

Vigile: Sì pronto mi dica.

Fabio: Sì, ecco, ho appena avuto un'incidente. Sono su via Magliana. Una ragazza non si è fermata allo stop e mi ha preso in pieno. Abbiamo bisogno di assistenza. Le due macchine sono completamente distrutte e non possiamo rimuoverle.

Vigile: Ho capito. Ci sono feriti?

Fabio: Sì, la ragazza.

Vigile: E' ferita gravemente?

Fabio: No, si è fatta male a una gamba. Forse è rotta, è appena arrivata l'ambulanza per portarla all'ospedale.

Vigile: Lei come sta?

Fabio: Io sto bene. Però le macchine in mezzo alla strada hanno bloccato il traffico. Devo chiamare il carro attrezzi?

Vigile: No, non dovete muovere le macchine. Aspettateci. La posizione delle macchine è importante per capire chi ha ragione e chi ha torto.

Fabio: Ho capito.

Vigile: Aspetti, chiamo la volante più vicina, sarà da voi tra pochissimo.

Fabio: Ok grazie.

Italian Conversation 25. Problemi, Reclami

Learn to understand spoken Italian better with our 'Italian Conversation' series.

Listen to the track below. Try to work out who is speaking and what about. You should listen several times.

If you have time, make notes on details of the conversation. You could even try it as a dictation!

Only when you've understood as much as you can, scroll down the page to check the transcript.

Transcript

25. Problemi, Reclami

Cliente: Salve, questo è l'ufficio reclami delle ferrovie?

Impiegato: Sì salve, mi dica pure.

Cliente: Volevo fare un reclamo. Il mio treno oggi ha avuto più di due ore di ritardo. Così ho perso anche la coincidenza e ora non posso tornare a casa. Vorrei il rimborso del biglietto.

Impiegato: Ho capito, che treno era?

Cliente: Era il treno delle 12 e 50 da Roma a Firenze. Doveva arrivare alle 15 ma è arrivato alle 17 passate. La coincidenza era alle 16 e 30.

Impiegato: D'accordo, deve compilare il modulo di reclamo. Il rimborso verrà fatto entro novanta giorni.

Cliente: Così tanto?

Impiegato: Purtroppo sono le regole dell'azienda, mi dispiace.

—

Cliente: Pronto, parlo con il servizio clienti di Compra.it?

Impiegato: Sì mi dica.

Cliente: Salve, vorrei fare un reclamo. La macchina fotografica che ho comprato sul vostro sito non funziona.

Impiegato: Allora, può mandarla indietro e noi le rimborsiamo i soldi. Deve incartare la macchinetta fotografica e rispedircela. Appena arriva, vi restituiremo i soldi sulla vostra carta di credito.

Cliente: Ho capito, grazie, a risentirci.

Section (D): Italian Short Story

Maui Pulls Up the Islands

One day Maui said to his four brothers, "Come fishing with me today! Let's go far out to sea. The fish are much bigger and better there, than they are close to land."

"Okay!" said his brothers. They were good fishermen and wanted those big fish. The four brothers and Maui jumped into their canoe and started to row. When they got far out to sea and could no longer see land, Maui jumped onto the end of the canoe. He drew out his magical fishing hook. When his brothers were looking ahead, he cast the hook over the side of the canoe. The hook sunk down deep into the blue water.

When his brothers were not looking, he cast his hook into the blue waters.

Soon, the magical hook stuck fast to the bottom of the sea. Maui pulled the fishing line tight. He called out, "See that tug? I must have hooked a giant fish!"

"Wow, I see that!" said one brother.

"That is some fish you caught!" said another.

"My brothers!" Maui called out. "Paddle hard so we can bring up this great fish!"

The brothers paddled with all their might. They paddled so hard they did not see that the hook was pulling up the land from the bottom of the sea. Behind them, one island after another rose from the sea!

Legend says that is how Maui made the islands, where the people now live.

Maui Catches the Sun

One day, Maui wanted to see how life was for the people who lived on the islands. But what he saw there made his heart skip a beat. Life was very hard for them. And he could see why - the days were just too short! There was not time in a day for people to do what they needed to do, like making and cooking food. If they laid out a wet blanket on the sand, the blanket would still be wet the next day. There was not even time for the fruit in the trees to get ripe.

"It is that Sun!" said Maui. "He is racing too fast across the sky! He is not thinking about the people who live down below, on the islands."

Maui knew it was up to him, a demi-god, to slow down the Sun. But how? He asked his brothers. He asked his sister Hina. He asked still others that he knew.

"Who do you think you are, Maui?" said one. "No one can catch the Sun!"

"Even if you are a demi-god," said another, "you know very well the Sun is too big and bright for anyone to stop."

Maui knew it was up to him, a demi-god, to slow down the Sun.

But Maui's sister Hina did not say these sorts of things. She cut off her long hair. She tied the hair into ropes and gave the ropes to Maui. From those ropes, Maui made a giant lasso.

That night, Maui took his lasso up to the very tallest mountain on the islands of Hawaii. The mountain had once been an active volcano. Years ago it had sent out waves of hot lava. When the volcano was over, a big crater was left at the top of the mountain. And that crater is where Maui planned to catch the Sun.

By the crater Maui waited, very still. He hid the lasso behind him, out of view. When the Sun rose at dawn, it started to race across the sky very fast. Soon that Sun was flying over the mountaintop. Brave Maui flung the lasso over his head. The ropes caught! The Sun tried and tried to move, but was trapped!

"Get me out of here!" shouted the Sun.

"Not yet!" said Maui. "You are moving too fast across the sky. It makes the days too short for the humans who live down below."

The Sun tried and tried to move, but it was trapped!

"So I like to go fast!" said the Sun. "Who cares? Let me out of here!"

"No!" said Maui in a big voice. "I care! You have to stay here, in this crater!" He pulled the lasso tight. But in his heart, Maui did not feel brave. He did not know how much longer he could hold on. True, his lasso was stronger than any other rope in all the land. But he did not know how long even a lasso made from his sister's hair could last before the hot rays of the Sun would burn it up.

The Sun tried to move again, but could not. "Oh, very well!" the Sun said, at last. You can be sure Maui was very glad to hear that! "I suppose I could slow down a little," said the Sun. "But only for part of the year."

So Maui and the Sun worked out a deal. For half the year, the Sun would move at a slow pace. Those days would be long, and that would be the summer. For the other half of the year, the sun could run as fast as it wanted to do. Those days would be short, and that would be the winter.

This is how Maui made the days longer for the people of the islands. At last, they could do the tasks they needed to do. They could have a full dinner and rest after. And the fruits on the trees grew big and sweet.

Translation to Italian:

Un giorno Maui disse ai suoi quattro fratelli: "Vieni a pescare con me oggi! Andiamo lontano dal mare, il pesce è molto più grande e migliore di quanto non sia vicino alla terra. "

"Ok!" Disse i suoi fratelli. Erano buoni pescatori e volevano questi pesci grossi. I quattro fratelli e Maui saltarono sulla loro canoa e iniziarono a remare. Quando andarono al mare e non riuscirono più a vedere la terraferma, Maui saltò sull'estremità della canoa. Tirò fuori il suo gancio magico. Mentre i suoi fratelli guardavano avanti, gettò il gancio sul lato della barca. Il gancio affondò in profondità nell'acqua blu.

Quando i suoi fratelli non guardarono, gettò il suo amo nelle acque blu.
Presto l'amo magico si aggrappa al fondo del mare, maui ha stretto la lenza. Gridò: "Vedi quel rimorchiatore? Devo aver appeso un pesce gigante!"
"Caspita, lo vedo!" Disse un fratello.
"È il pesce che hai catturato!" dice un altro.
"Fratelli miei!" Chiamato Maui. "Rema duramente per poter allevare questo bellissimo pesce!"
I fratelli remarono con tutte le loro forze. Hanno remato così tanto che non hanno visto che l'amo stava tirando la terra dal fondo del mare: dietro di loro, un'isola dopo l'altra è andata via dal mare!
La leggenda dice che così Maui creò le isole, dove ora vivono le persone.

Maui prende il sole

Un giorno, Maui voleva vedere com'era la vita degli abitanti delle isole. Ma quello che vide lì gli fece battere il cuore. La vita è stata molto dura per loro. E capì perché - i giorni erano troppo brevi! Durante il giorno, le persone non hanno avuto il tempo di fare ciò che dovevano fare, come cucinare e cucinare. Se stendessero una coperta bagnata sulla sabbia, sarebbe comunque bagnata il giorno successivo. Non c'è nemmeno il tempo di maturare il frutto tra gli alberi"È quel sole!" Disse Maui. "Corre troppo veloce nel cielo! Non pensa alle persone che vivono nelle isole."
Maui sapeva che dipendeva da lui, un semidio, rallentare il sole. Ma come? Chiese ai suoi fratelli. Chiese a sua sorella Hina. Ha chiesto ad altre persone che conosceva.
"Chi sei, Maui?" Disse uno di loro. "Nessuno può prendere il sole!"
"Anche se sei un semidio," disse un altro, "sai benissimo che il sole è troppo grande e troppo luminoso perché qualcuno si fermi lì.
Maui sapeva che dipendeva da lui, un semidio, rallentare il sole.

Ma la sorella di Maui, Hina, non ha detto questo genere di cose. Si tagliò i capelli lunghi. Legò i capelli alle corde e li porse a Maui. Maui fece un lazo gigante da queste corde. Quella notte, Maui portò il suo lazo sulla montagna più alta delle Isole Hawaii. La montagna era già stata un vulcano attivo. Anni fa, aveva inviato ondate di lava calda. Alla fine del vulcano, rimaneva un grande cratere in cima alla montagna. E questo cratere è dove Maui ha pianificato di prendere il sole. Al cratere, Maui attese, immobile. Si nascose il lazo dietro di sé, fuori dalla vista. Quando il sole sorse all'alba, corse molto veloce nel cielo. Presto questo sole volò in cima alla montagna. Il coraggioso Maui gli gettò il lazo in testa. Le corde catturate! Il sole tentò e si mosse, ma fu intrappolato!
"Portami fuori di qui!" Gridò il sole.
"Non ancora!" Disse Maui. "Stai andando troppo veloce nel cielo. Questo rende i giorni troppo brevi per gli umani che vivono al piano di sotto."
Il sole ha provato e cercato di muoversi, ma era intrappolato!
"Quindi mi piace andare veloce! Disse il sole. "Non ci interessa, fammi uscire di qui!"

"No!" Disse Maui con una gran voce. "Sono preoccupato, devi stare qui in questo cratere!" Strinse il lazo, ma nel suo cuore Maui non si sentì coraggioso. Non sapeva per quanto tempo poteva restare. Certamente, il suo lazo era più forte di qualsiasi altra corda in tutto il paese. Ma non sapeva per quanto tempo poteva durare un lazo fatto dai capelli di sua sorella prima che i raggi ardenti del sole lo bruciassero.

Il sole tentò di muoversi di nuovo, ma non ci riuscì. "Oh, molto bene!" Detto il sole, finalmente. Puoi essere sicuro che Maui è stato molto felice di saperlo! "Immagino di poter rallentare un po'" disse il sole. "Ma solo per una parte dell'anno."

Quindi Maui e il Sole hanno raggiunto un accordo. Durante la metà dell'anno, il sole si muoveva lentamente. In questi giorni sarebbe lungo e sarebbe estate. Durante l'altra metà dell'anno, il sole poteva correre più veloce che voleva. In questi giorni sarebbe breve e sarebbe inverno.

Fu così che Maui prolungò i giorni degli isolani. Alla fine, potevano svolgere i compiti di cui avevano bisogno. Potrebbero cenare e riposarsi dopo. E i frutti sugli alberi sono diventati grandi e dolci.

www.ingramcontent.com/pod-product-compliance
Lightning Source LLC
Chambersburg PA
CBHW081419080526
44589CB00016B/2601